Letters to a Young Novelist

Letters to a Young Novelist

MARIO VARGAS LLOSA

TRANSLATED BY NATASHA WIMMER

Farrar, Straus and Giroux

New York

Farrar, Straus and Giroux
19 Union Square West, New York 10003

Distributed in Canada by Douglas & McIntyre Ltd.
Printed in the United States of America
Originally published in 1997 by Ariel/Planeta, Spain, as
Cartas a un joven novelista
Published in the United States by Farrar, Straus and Giroux
First American edition, 2002

Portions of this book have appeared in *Literary Review*, *Partisan Review*, *Tin House*, and *The Yale Review*.

ISBN: 0-374-11916-3
Library of Congress Control Number: 2002101065

Designed by Jonathan D. Lippincott

www.fsgbooks.com

1 3 5 7 9 10 8 6 4 2

Contents

Letters to a Young Novelist

The Parable of the Tapeworm

DEAR FRIEND,

I was moved by your letter because in it I saw myself at fourteen or fifteen, in gray Lima under the dictatorship of General Odría, aflame with the desire to one day become a writer yet disheartened because I didn't know what steps to take, how to begin channeling my ambition, which I experienced as an urgent prompting, into the creation of real works; how to write stories that would dazzle my readers as I had been dazzled by the writers I was beginning to install in my personal pantheon: Faulkner, Hemingway, Malraux, Dos Passos, Camus, Sartre.

Many times it occurred to me to write to one of them (they were all still alive) and ask for their advice on how to be a writer. I never dared, out of shyness or out of the kind of defeatism — why write, if I know no one will deign to respond? — that so often thwarts the ambitions of young people in countries where literature means little to most and survives on the margins of society as an almost underground activity.

You do not suffer from that kind of paralysis, since you've written to me. That's a fine beginning to the adventure you wish to set out on and from which you expect—as I'm sure you do, though you don't tell me so in your letter—many marvelous things. I venture to suggest that you not expect quite so much and that you not count too much on success. There's no reason why you shouldn't be successful, of course, but if you persevere in writing and publishing, you'll soon discover that prizes, public acclaim, book sales, the social standing of a writer all have a sui generis appeal; they are extraordinarily arbitrary, sometimes stubbornly evading those who most deserve them while besieging and overwhelming those who merit them least. Which means that those who see success as their main goal will probably never realize their dreams; they are confusing literary ambition with a hunger for glory and for the financial gains that literature affords certain writers (very few of them). There is a difference.

The defining characteristic of the literary vocation may be that those who possess it experience the exercise of their craft as its own best reward, much superior to anything they might gain from the fruits of their labors. That is one thing I am sure of amid my many uncertainties regarding the literary vocation: deep inside, a writer feels that writing is the best thing that ever happened to him, or could ever happen to him, because as far as he is concerned, writing is the best possible way of life, never mind the social, political, or financial rewards of what he might achieve through it.

Vocation seems to me the inevitable starting point for our talk about what is exciting and troubling you: namely, how to become a writer. It's a mysterious business, of course, veiled in doubt and subjectivity. But that doesn't stop us from trying to explain it rationally, rejecting the religious fervor and pride of the self-important myths the romantics spun around it, according to which the writer was the chosen one of the gods, a being singled out by a transcendent superhuman entity to write divine words that, once breathed, would effect the sublimation of the human soul and allow the writer, thanks to his brush with Beauty (capitalized, of course), to achieve immortality.

Today nobody talks that way about literary or artistic vocation, but even though the definition offered in our times is less grandiose, less steeped in fatefulness, it is still fairly elusive: a predisposition of murky origin that causes certain men and women to dedicate their lives to an activity that one day they feel called, almost obliged, to pursue, because they sense that only in pursuing this vocation—writing stories, for example—will they feel complete, at peace with themselves, able to give the best of themselves without the nagging fear that they are wasting their lives.

I don't believe that the destinies of human beings are programmed in the womb by fate or by a mischievous divinity that distributes aptitudes, ineptitudes, likes, and dislikes among brand-new souls. But neither do I believe, as once I did under the influence of the French existentialists—especially Sartre—that vocation is a *choice*, a free expression of individual will that decides a person's future. Indeed, in spite of my conviction that literary vocation is not governed by fate or inscribed in the genes of future writers, and despite my belief that discipline and perseverance may sometimes produce genius, I've come to be convinced that it cannot be explained solely in terms of free choice. Free choice is essential, in my opinion, but only at a second stage, following an initial subjective inclination, innate or forged in childhood or earliest adolescence, that rational choice serves to strengthen but is unable to manufacture from scratch.

If I'm not mistaken in my supposition (though I very well may be), a man or a woman develops precociously in childhood or early in his or her teenage years a penchant for dreaming up people, situations, anecdotes, worlds different from the world in which he or she lives, and that inclination is the first sign of what may later be termed literary vocation. Naturally, there is an abyss that the vast majority of human beings never cross between the propensity to retreat from the real world and real life into the imagination and the actual practice of literature. Those who do cross and who become creators of worlds with the written word are writers, the minority who have reinforced their penchant or tendency with an exertion of the will Sartre called *choice*. At a given moment, they decided to become writers. That's what they chose to be. They arranged their lives to make the written word the focus of the drive that at first they contented themselves with harnessing for the elaboration, in the misty realms of the mind, of other lives and worlds. This is where you are now: at the difficult and thrilling moment when you must decide whether you will go beyond amusing yourself with the creation of fictional realities, whether you will set them down in writing. If that's what you choose, you will certainly have taken a very important step, though your future as a writer will still be far from assured. But the decision to commit yourself, to orient your life toward the achievement of your purposes, is already a way—the only possible way—of beginning to be a writer.

What is the origin of this early inclination, the source of the literary vocation, for inventing beings and stories? The answer, I think, is rebellion. I'm convinced that those who immerse themselves in the lucubration of lives different from their own demonstrate indirectly their rejection and criticism of life as it is, of the real world, and manifest their desire to substitute for it the creations of their imagination and dreams. Why would anyone who is deeply satisfied with reality, with real life as it is lived, dedicate himself to something as insubstantial and fanciful as the creation of fictional realities? Naturally, those who rebel against life as it is, using their ability to invent different lives and different people, may do so for any number of reasons, honorable or dishonorable, generous or selfish, complex or banal. The nature of this basic questioning of reality, which to my mind lies at the heart of every literary calling, doesn't matter at all. What matters is that the rejection be strong enough to fuel the enthusiasm for a task as quixotic as tilting at windmills—the sleight-of-hand replacement of the concrete, objective world of life as it is lived with the subtle and ephemeral world of fiction.

Nevertheless, despite the evanescence of fiction, and the subjective, figurative, extrahistorical nature of its execution, it comes to have long-term effects on the real world—in other words, on the lives of flesh-and-blood people.

This questioning of real life, which is the secret raison d'être of literature—of the literary vocation—ensures that literature offers a unique vision of a given period. Life as described in fiction (especially in superior fiction) is never just life as it was lived by those who imagined, wrote, read, or experienced it but rather the fictional equivalent, what they were obliged to fabricate because they weren't able to live it in reality and, as a result, resigned themselves to live only in the indirect and subjective way it could be lived: in dreams and in fiction. Fiction is a lie covering up a deep truth: it is life as it wasn't, life as the men and women of a certain age wanted to live it and didn't and thus had to invent. It isn't the face of History but rather her reverse or flip side: what didn't happen and therefore had to be fabricated in the imagination and in words to fulfill the ambitions real life was unable to satisfy, to fill the voids women and men discovered around them and tried to populate with ghosts they conjured up themselves.

This rebellion is relative, of course. Many story writers aren't even conscious of it, and it's possible that if they were to become aware of the seditious roots of their calling, they would be surprised and frightened since in their public lives they certainly don't imagine themselves as plotting secretly to dynamite the world they inhabit. On the other hand, theirs is ultimately a fairly peaceful rebellion. What harm is there, after all, in pitting vaporous fictional lives against real life? Where is the danger in such a contest? At first glance, there is none. It's just a game, isn't it? And games aren't supposed to be dangerous, so long as they don't threaten to overflow their boundaries and mingle with real life. Of course, when a person—Don Quixote or Madame Bovary, for example—insists on confusing fiction with life and tries to make life resemble fiction, the consequences can be disastrous. Those who behave in such a way tend to suffer terrible disappointments.

So the game of literature is not innocuous. The fruit of a deep dissatisfaction with real life, fiction is itself a source of discomfort and dissatisfaction. Those who, through reading, *live* a great story—like the two tales I've just referred to, by Cervantes and Flaubert—return to real life with a heightened sensitivity to its limitations and imperfections, alerted by these magnificent fantasies to the fact that the real world, and life as it is lived, is infinitely more mediocre than life as invented by novelists. When readers are faced with the real world, the unease fomented by good literature may, in certain circumstances, even translate itself into an act of rebellion against authority, the establishment, or sanctioned beliefs.

That's why the Spanish Inquisition distrusted works of fiction and subjected them to strict censorship, going so far as to prohibit them in the American colonies for three hundred years. The pretext was that these wild tales might distract the Indians from the worship of God, the only serious concern of a theocratic society. Like the Inquisition, all governments and regimes aspiring to control the life of their citizens have shown a similar distrust of fiction and have submitted it to the kind of scrutiny and pruning called censorship. None of these authorities have been mistaken: innocent as it may seem, the writing of stories is a way of exercising freedom and of quarreling with those—religious or secular—who wish to do away with it. That's why all dictatorships—fascist, communist, or Islamic fundamentalist regimes, African or Latin American military tyrannies—have tried to control literature by forcing it into the straitjacket of censorship.

But these general reflections have caused us to stray a little from your particular case. Let's get back to specifics. Deep down, you've felt a certain predilection, and you've bolstered it with an exertion of will and decided to devote yourself to literature. Now what?

Your decision to claim your literary leanings as your destiny must lead you into servitude, into nothing less than slavery. To put it graphically, you've just done what some nineteenth-century ladies, concerned about their weight and determined to recover their slender silhouettes, were reputed to do: you've swallowed a tapeworm. Have you ever come across anyone who sheltered that terrible parasite in his gut? I have, and I assure you those ladies were heroines, martyrs to beauty. In the early sixties in Paris, a great friend of mine, José María, a young Spanish painter and filmmaker, was invaded by such a creature. Once the tapeworm establishes itself inside an organism, it merges with it, feeds off it, grows and is nourished at its expense; the worm is very difficult to expel from the body it thrives on and effectively colonizes.

José María kept getting thinner, even though he was constantly forced to eat and drink (milk, especially) to satisfy the gnawing of the creature housed inside him, since if he didn't, his suffering would become intolerable. But everything he ate and drank was for the tapeworm's benefit, not his. One day, when we were talking in a little Montparnasse bistro, he surprised me with the following confession: "We do so many things together. We go to theaters, exhibitions, bookstores, we spend hours and hours discussing politics, books, films, friends. And you think I do these things for the same reason you do, because I enjoy them. But you're wrong. I do them all for it, for the tapeworm. That's how it seems to me: that my whole life is lived no longer for my sake but for the sake of what I carry inside me, of which I am now no more than a servant."

Ever since then, I've liked to compare the lot of the writer to that of my friend José María when he had the tapeworm inside him. The literary vocation is not a hobby, a sport, a pleasant leisure-time activity. It is an all-encompassing, all-excluding occupation, an urgent priority, a freely chosen servitude that turns its victims (its lucky victims) into slaves. Like José María's tapeworm, literature becomes a permanent preoccupation, something that takes up your entire existence, that overflows the hours you devote to writing and seeps into everything else you do, because the literary vocation feeds off the life of the writer just as the tapeworm feeds off the bodies it invades. As Flaubert said: "Writing is just another way of living." In other words, those who make this enchanting and engrossing vocation their own don't write to live but live to write.

This idea of comparing the writer's vocation to a tapeworm is not original. I've just come across it reading Thomas Wolfe, who described his vocation as the lodging of a worm in his very being:

> For sleep was dead forever, the merciful, dark and sweet oblivions of childhood sleep. The worm had entered at my heart, the worm lay coiled and feeding at my brain, my spirit, and my memory—I knew that finally I had been caught in my own fire, consumed by my own hungers, impaled on the hook of that furious and insensate desire that had absorbed my life for years. I knew, in short, that one bright cell in the brain or heart or memory would now blaze on forever—by night, by day, through every waking, sleeping moment of my life, the worm would feed and the light be lit,—that no anodyne of food or drink, or friendship, travel, sport or woman could ever quench it, and that never more until death put its total and conclusive darkness on my life, could I escape.
>
> I knew at last I had become a writer: I knew at last what happens to a man who makes the writer's life his own.*

*"The Story of a Novelist," *The Autobiography of an American Novelist*, ed. Leslie Field (Cambridge, Mass.: Harvard U. Press, 1983), pp. 68–69.

I think that only those who come to literature as they might to religion, prepared to dedicate their time, energy, and efforts to their vocation, have what it takes to really become writers and transcend themselves in their works. The mysterious thing we call talent, or genius, does not spring to life full-fledged—at least not in novelists, although it may sometimes in poets or musicians (the classic examples being Rimbaud and Mozart, of course). Instead it becomes apparent at the end of many long years of discipline and perseverance. There are no novel-writing prodigies. All the greatest, most revered novelists were first apprentice writers whose budding talent required early application and conviction. The example of those writers who, unlike Rimbaud, a brilliant poet even as an adolescent, were required to cultivate their talent gives heart to the beginner, don't you think?

If you are interested in the subject—the fostering of literary genius—I recommend that you read the voluminous correspondence of Flaubert, and especially the letters he wrote to his lover, Louise Colet, between 1850 and 1854, the period in which he wrote *Madame Bovary*, his first masterpiece. I read them while I was writing my first books, and they were very helpful. Although Flaubert was a misanthrope and his letters are full of tirades against humanity, his love for literature was boundless. That is why he pledged himself to his vocation like a crusader, surrendering himself to it day and night, working with fanatical conviction, pushing to surpass himself. In this way, he managed to overcome his limitations (very evident in his early works, which are as formal and ornate as the romantic models then in fashion) and write novels like *Madame Bovary* and *A Sentimental Education*, perhaps the first two modern novels.

Another book you might read on the subject addressed by this letter is one by William S. Burroughs, a very different kind of author: *Junky*. Burroughs doesn't interest me at all as a novelist: his experimental, psychedelic stories have always bored me, so much so that I don't think I've ever been able to finish one. But *Junky*, the first book he wrote, a factual and autobiographical account of how he became a drug addict and how his addiction to drugs—free choice augmenting what was already doubtless a certain proclivity—made him a willing slave, furnishes an accurate description of what I believe to be the literary vocation, of the utter interdependence of the writer and his work and the way the latter feeds on the former, on all he is and does or does not do.

But, my friend, this letter has gone on longer than it should, belonging as it does to a genre—the epistolary—of which the primary virtue is precisely brevity, and so I'll take my leave.

Fondly,

The *Catoblepas*

DEAR FRIEND,

I've been so busy in the last few days that I haven't written back as soon as I should have, but I've been thinking about your letter ever since I received it. Not only because I share its enthusiasm, believing as you do that literature is the best thing ever invented to combat misfortune, but also because the questions you ask—"Where do stories come from?" and "How do novelists come up with their ideas?"—still intrigue me as much as they did in the early days of my literary apprenticeship, even now that I've written a good many novels.

I have an answer for you, which will have to be very nuanced if it is not to be entirely false. All stories are rooted in the lives of those who write them; experience is the source from which fiction flows. This doesn't mean, of course, that novels are always thinly disguised biographies of their authors; rather, that in every fiction, even the most freely imagined, it is possible to uncover a starting point, a secret node viscerally linked to the experiences of the writer. I'd venture to claim that there are no exceptions to this rule and that, as a result, scientifically pure invention does not exist in literature. All fictions are structures of fantasy and craft erected around certain acts, people, or circumstances that stand out in the writer's memory and stimulate his imagination, leading him to create a world so rich and various that sometimes it is almost impossible (and sometimes just plain impossible) to recognize in it the autobiographical material that was its genesis and that is, in a way, the secret heart of all fiction, as well as its obverse and antithesis.

At a youth conference, I tried to explain this process as a backwards striptease. Writing novels is the equivalent of what professional strippers do when they take off their clothes and exhibit their naked bodies on stage. The novelist performs the same acts in reverse. In constructing the novel, he goes through the motions of getting dressed, hiding the nudity in which he began under heavy, multicolored articles of clothing conjured up out of his imagination. The process is so complex and exacting that many times not even the author is able to identify in the finished product—that exuberant display of his ability to invent imaginary people and worlds—the images lurking in his memory, fixed there by life, which sparked his imagination, spurred him on, and induced him to produce his story.

As for themes, well, I believe the novelist feeds off himself, like the *catoblepas*, the mythical animal that appears to Saint Anthony in Flaubert's *The Temptation of Saint Anthony* and that Borges later revisited in his *Book of Imaginary Beings*. The *catoblepas* is an impossible creature that devours itself, beginning with its feet. Likewise, the novelist scavenges his own experience for raw material for stories—in a more abstract sense, of course. He does this not just in order to re-create characters, anecdotes, or landscapes from the stuff of certain memories but also to gather fuel from them for the willpower that must sustain him if he is to see the long, hard project through.

I'll venture a little further in discussing the themes of fiction. The novelist doesn't choose his themes; he is chosen by them. He writes on certain subjects because certain things have happened to him. In the choice of a theme, the writer's freedom is relative, perhaps even nonexistent. In any case, it is nothing when compared with his freedom to choose the literary form of his work; there, it seems to me, he enjoys total liberty—and total responsibility. My impression is that life—a big word, I know—inflicts themes on a writer through certain experiences that impress themselves on his consciousness or subconscious and later compel him to shake himself free by turning them into stories. We need hardly seek out examples of the way themes from life thrust themselves on writers, because all testimonies tend to concur: a story, a character, a situation, a mystery haunted me, obsessed me, importuned me from the very depths of my self until I was obliged to write it to be free of it. Of course, Proust's is the first name that comes to anyone's mind. A real writer-*catoblepas*, wasn't he? Who ever consumed themselves more thoroughly or profitably, digging like an archaeologist in all the nooks and crannies of memory, than the industrious creator of *In Search of Lost Time*, that monumental artistic re-creation of Proust's daily life, family, surroundings, friendships, relationships, speakable or unspeakable appetites, likes, and dislikes — and, at the same time, of the subtle and mysterious charms of the human spirit in its painstaking efforts to collect, sort, unearth and bury, associate and dissociate, polish, or deface the images that memory retains of time past. Proust's biographers (Painter, for example) have been able to come up with long lists of real experiences and people concealed in the sumptuous inventions of the Proustian saga, demonstrating beyond a doubt that this prodigious literary creation was assembled out of raw materials from the life of its author. But what those lists of autobiographical data unearthed by the critics really prove to us is something else: the creative capacity of Proust, who, exploiting his introspection and his immersion in the past, transformed the incidents of his fairly conventional existence into a splendid tapestry, a stunning representation of the human condition perceived from the point of view of a consciousness turned inward to view the unfolding of life itself.

This brings us to another realization, no less important than the previous one. Although the starting point of a novelist's invention is what he has lived, that is not, and cannot be, its ending point. The invention's end is located at a considerable distance — sometimes a cosmic distance — from its origin, because as a theme is embodied in language and narrative, the autobiographical material is transformed, enriched (sometimes leached of value), integrated with other remembered or invented materials, and manipulated and structured—if the novel is a real creation—until it achieves the complete autonomy that fiction must assume to live of its own accord. (Those stories that never cast off from their authors and that serve only as biographical documents are, of course, failed fictions.) The task of the novelist is to transform the material supplied by his own memory into an objective world constructed of words: the novel. Form is what allows the text to cohere, to take concrete shape; and it is in the manipulation of form, if my conception of the literary project is correct (and I repeat, I have my doubts), that the novelist enjoys complete freedom and therefore responsibility for his results. If what you are reading between the lines is that, in my opinion, fiction writers are not responsible for their themes (since life assigns them) but are responsible for the way they convert them into literature and that as a result it is possible to say that they are ultimately responsible for their success or failure—for their mediocrity or genius—that is indeed exactly what I mean to say.

Why, of all the infinite occurrences in a writer's life, do some stimulate creativity so vigorously and so many others filter through the memory without rousing the imagination? I don't know for sure. All I have is a suspicion. And that is that the faces, anecdotes, situations, and conflicts that impress themselves on a writer and lead him to dream up stories are precisely those representing that dissent from real life, from the world as it is, which, as I noted in my previous letter, is the root of the novelist's vocation, the hidden impulse that drives him to defy the real world by replacing it symbolically with fiction.

Of the many examples that might be cited to illustrate this idea, I choose that of a minor writer—though he was prolific to the point of incontinence—of eighteenth-century France, Restif de la Bretonne. I don't choose him for his talent—he didn't have much—but for the clear-cut nature of his particular rebellion against reality, his discomfort in the real world, which drove him to engineer fictional realities designed to mimic the world as he would have liked it to be.

In the many novels written by Restif de la Bretonne (the best known is his lengthy novelistic autobiography, *Monsieur Nicolas*) eighteenth-century France, rural and urban, is documented by a painstaking sociologist and rigorous observer of human types, customs, daily routines, work, festivals, superstitions, attire, and beliefs, in such a way that his books have become a veritable treasure trove for researchers: historians, anthropologists, ethnologists, and sociologists have helped themselves liberally to the information excavated by the tireless Restif from the quarry of his era. Nevertheless, in being transposed into his novels, this social and historical realism so copiously described undergoes a radical transformation, and that is why it is possible to speak of the novels as fiction. In the teeming world he creates, similar in so many details to the real world that inspired it, men fall in love with women not for the beauty of their faces, the slenderness of their waists, their good breeding, or spiritual charms but ultimately for the beauty of their feet or the elegance of their boots. Restif de la

Bretonne was a fetishist, something that in real life made him an eccentric among his contemporaries, an exception to the rule, that is to say, a "dissident" from reality. And that dissidence, surely the driving force of his vocation, is revealed to us in his works, in which life is corrected, reworked in the image and likeness of Restif himself. In the world as Restif experienced it, it was natural and normal that the principal female attribute, the object of pleasure coveted by men—*all* men—should be that delicate extremity and, by extension, its coverings, stockings and shoes. Few writers make it possible to grasp so plainly the process by which fiction transforms the world through the subjective urges—desires, appetites, dreams, frustrations, grudges, et cetera—of novelists as this instructive Frenchman.

All creators of fiction are embroiled in the same process, though less thoroughly and blatantly. There is something in their lives like the fetishism of Restif—a noble craving for justice, an egotistical drive to satisfy the most sordid masochistic or sadistic urges, a reasonable human longing to live a life of adventure, an undying love—that makes them wish passionately for a world different from the one they live in, a world that they are then compelled to construct of words and upon which they stamp, usually in code, their questioning of real life and their affirmation of that other reality which their selfishness or generosity spurs them to set up in place of the one they've been allotted.

Perhaps, my budding young novelist friend, this is the right moment to speak of a notion dangerous when it is applied to literature: authenticity. What does it mean to be an authentic writer? What is certain is that fiction is, by definition, fraud—something that is not real yet pretends to be—and that all novels are lies passing themselves off as truth, creations whose *power of persuasion* depends entirely on the novelist's skill at performing conjuring and sleight-of-hand tricks, like a circus or theater magician. So does it make sense to speak of authenticity in fiction, a genre in which it is most authentic to be a trickster, a swindler? It does, but in this way: the authentic novelist is the novelist who docilely obeys the rules life dictates, writing on those themes born out of experience and possessed of urgency and avoiding all others. That is what authenticity or sincerity is for the novelist: the acceptance of his own demons and the decision to serve them as well as possible.

The novelist who doesn't write about what deep down stimulates and inspires him and who coldly chooses subjects or themes in a rational manner because he believes that way he'll have a better chance at success is inauthentic and most likely a bad novelist (even if he is successful—the best-seller lists are crowded with very bad novelists, as you are well aware). But it seems unlikely to me that anyone will become a creator—a transformer of reality—if he doesn't write encouraged and nourished from the depths of his being by those ghosts (or demons) who've made us novelists determined protesters and reconstructors of life in the stories we tell. I think that to accept that imposition—to write about what obsesses us and excites us and is viscerally though often

22

mysteriously part of our lives—is to write "better," with more conviction and energy, and to be better equipped to undertake the exciting but also arduous and sometimes disappointing and harrowing task of composing a novel.

Those writers who shun their own demons and set themselves themes because they believe their own aren't original or appealing enough are making an enormous mistake. In and of itself, no literary theme is good or bad. Any themes can be either, and the verdict depends not on the theme itself but rather on what it becomes when the application of form—narrative style and structure—makes it a novel. It is the form a theme is couched in that makes a story original or trivial, profound or superficial, complex or simple; that lends its characters depth, ambiguity, credibility or turns them into lifeless caricatures, the creations of a puppet master. That is another of the few rules of literature that, it seems to me, brook no exceptions: the themes of a novel themselves promise nothing, because they'll be judged good or bad, appealing or dull solely in view of what the novelist does to turn them into a reality of words ranged in a certain order.

Well, my friend, I think that's all for now.

Fondly,

The Power of Persuasion

Dear Friend,

You're right. My first few letters, with their vague hypothesizing on the literary vocation and the origin of novelists' themes, not to mention their zoological allegories—the tapeworm, the *catoblepas*—were overly abstract, their suppositions sadly unverifiable. Which means that the moment has come for us to move on to less subjective matters, ones more specifically rooted in literary practice.

Let us speak, then, of form, which, paradoxical as it may seem, is the novel's most concrete attribute, since it is form that gives novels their shape and substance. But before we set sail on waters so alluring for those who, like you and me, love and practice the narrative craft, it's worth establishing what you already know very well, though it is not so clear to most readers of novels: the separation of form and content (or theme and style and narrative structure) is artificial, admissible only when we are explaining or analyzing them; it never occurs in reality, since the story a novel tells is inseparable from the way it is told. This *way* is what determines whether the tale is believable or not, moving or ridiculous, comic or dramatic. It is of course possible to say that *Moby-Dick* is the story of a sea captain obsessed with a white whale that he pursues across all the world's oceans and that *Don Quixote* tells of the adventures and misadventures of a half-mad knight who tries to reproduce on the plains of La Mancha the deeds of the heroes of chivalric literature. But would anyone who has read those novels recognize in such plot descriptions the infinitely rich and subtle universes of Melville and Cervantes? To explain the mechanisms that bring a tale to life, it is permissible to separate content from form only on the condition that it is made clear that such a division never occurs naturally, at least not in good novels. It does occur, on the other hand, in bad ones, and that is why they're bad, but in good novels what is told and the way it is told are inextricably bound up together. They are good because thanks to the effectiveness of their form they are endowed with an irresistible *power of persuasion*.

If before reading *The Metamorphosis* you had been told that it was about the transformation of a meek little office worker into a repulsive cockroach, you probably would have yawned and said to yourself there was no reason to read such a ridiculous tale. However, since you've read the story as Kafka magically tells it, you "believe" wholeheartedly in the terrible plight of Gregor Samsa: you identify with him, you suffer with him, and you feel choked by the same despair that destroys the poor character, until with his death the ordinariness of life as it was (before his unhappy adventure disturbed it) is restored. And you believe the story of Gregor Samsa because Kafka was capable of finding a way to tell it— in words, silences, revelations, details, organization of information and narrative flow—that overwhelms the reader's defenses, surmounting all the mental reservations he or she might harbor when faced with such a tale.

To equip a novel with *power of persuasion*, it is necessary to tell your story in such a way that it makes the most of every personal experience implicit in its plot and characters; at the same time, it must transmit to the reader an illusion of autonomy from the real world he inhabits. The more independent and self-contained a novel seems to us, and the more everything happening in it gives us the impression of occurring as a result of the story's internal mechanisms and not as a result of the arbitrary imposition of an outside will, the greater the novel's power of persuasion. When a novel gives us the impression of self-sufficiency, of being freed from *real* life, of containing in itself everything it requires to exist, it has reached its maximum capacity for persuasion, successfully seducing its readers and making them believe what it tells them. Good novels—great ones—never actually seem to tell us anything; rather, they make us live it and share in it by virtue of their persuasive powers.

You're undoubtedly familiar with Bertolt Brecht's famous theory of the alienation effect. He believed that to succeed in writing the kind of epic and didactic theater he proposed, it was essential to develop a way of staging plays— reflected in the movement or speech of the actors and even the construction of the sets—that would gradually destroy the "illusion" and remind the audience that what they were seeing was not real life but theater, a fabrication, a performance, from which, nevertheless, conclusions should be drawn and lessons learned promoting action and reform. I don't know what you think of Brecht. I believe he was a great writer, and that, although he was often hampered by his propagandistic and ideological aims, his plays are excellent and, thankfully, much more persuasive than his theorizing.

In its persuasive efforts, the novel aims for exactly the opposite effect: to reduce the distance that separates fiction from reality and, once that boundary is elided, to make the reader live the lie of fiction as if it were the most eternal truth, its illusions the most consistent and convincing depictions of reality. That is the trick great novels play: they convince us that the world is the way they describe it, as if fiction were not what it is, the picture of a world dismantled and rebuilt to satisfy the deicidal urge to remake reality, the urge that fuels the novelist's vocation whether he knows it or not. Only bad novels foster the alienation Brecht wanted his spectators to experience in order to learn the political lessons he meant to impart along with his plays. Bad novels lacking in the power of persuasion, or possessing only a weak strain of it, don't convince us that the lie they're telling is true; the "lie" appears to us as what it is: a construction, an arbitrary, lifeless invention that moves ploddingly and clumsily, like the puppets of a mediocre puppet master whose threads, manipulated by their creator, are in full sight, exposing them as caricatures of living beings. The deeds or sufferings of these caricatures will scarcely be able to move us: do they, after all, experience anything themselves? They are no more than captive shades, borrowed lives dependent on an omnipotent master.

Naturally, the autonomy of fiction is not a truth—it is a fiction, too. That is to say, fiction is autonomous only in a figurative sense, and that's why I've been very careful when referring to it to speak of an "illusion of autonomy," "the impression of self-sufficiency, of being freed from *real* life." *Someone* is writing these novels. That fact, that they are not the product of spontaneous generation, makes them dependent, connects each of them by an umbilical cord to the rest of the world. But it's not just having an author that links novels to real life; if the storytelling inventions of novels did not reflect on the world as it is lived by their readers, the novel would be something remote and mute, an artifice that shuts us out: it would never possess any power of persuasion, it could never cast a spell, seduce readers, convince them of its truth, and make them live what it relates as if they were experiencing it themselves.

This is the curious ambiguity of fiction: it must aspire to independence knowing that its slavery to reality is inevitable, and it must suggest through sophisticated techniques an autonomy and self-sufficiency as deceptive as the melodies of an opera divorced from the instruments or the throats that voice them.

Form works these miracles—when it works. It is in practical terms an indivisible entity, made up of two equally important components that, though they are always inter-twined, may be isolated for purposes of analysis and explica-tion: style and order. *Style* refers, of course, to words, to the way a story is written; *order* to the organization of the story's elements. To simplify greatly, order concerns the great axes of all novelistic construction: narrative space and time.

So as not to make this letter too long, I'll leave for next time some thoughts on *style*, the language of fiction, and the workings of that *power of persuasion* on which the life (or death) of all novels depends.

Fondly,

Style

Dear Friend,

Style is an essential element, though not the only element, of narrative form. Novels are made of words, which means that the way a writer chooses and orders his language largely determines whether his stories possess or lack the power of persuasion. Of course, a novel's language cannot be disassociated from what it relates—words shape their subject. The only way to know if a novelist has succeeded or failed in his narrative undertaking is to decide whether, through his writing, the fiction lives, liberates itself from its creator and real life, and impresses itself on the reader as an autonomous reality.

It is, therefore, what a text relates that determines whether it is efficient or inefficient, life-giving or lifeless. To identify the elements of style, perhaps we should begin by eliminating the idea of *correctness*. It doesn't matter at all whether a style is correct or incorrect; what matters is that it be efficient, or suited to its task, which is to endow the stories it tells with the illusion of life—real life. There are novelists who write very correctly, obeying the grammatical and stylistic imperatives of their times, like Cervantes, Stendhal, Dickens, García Márquez, and there are others, no less great, who break all the rules and make all kinds of grammatical mistakes, like Balzac, Joyce, Pío Baroja, Céline, Cortázar, and Lezama Lima. Their style is full of improprieties from the academic point of view, but that does not prevent them from being good or even excellent novelists. The Spanish writer Azorín, who was an extraordinary prose stylist (and nevertheless a very boring novelist), wrote in a collection of autobiographical essays titled *Madrid*: "The man of letters writes prose, correct prose, classical prose, and yet that prose is worth nothing without the leavening of grace, worthy intent, irony, disdain, or sarcasm." It is a sharp observation: on its own, stylistic correctness does not guarantee either the success or the failure of a work of fiction.

On what, then, does the success of a novel's language depend? On two qualities: its internal coherence and its essentiality. The story a novel tells can be incoherent, but the language that shapes it must be coherent if the incoherence is to be genuinely and convincingly simulated. An example of this is Molly Bloom's monologue at the end of Joyce's *Ulysses*, a chaotic torrent of memories, feelings, thoughts, and emotions. Its power to bewitch derives from a prose that is seemingly ragged and fragmented but that retains beneath its unruly and anarchic surface a rigorous coherence, a structural consistency that follows a model or original system of rules and principles from which it never deviates. Is the monologue an exact *description* of consciousness in motion? No. It is a literary creation so powerfully convincing that it seems to us to mimic the meandering of Molly's consciousness when really it is inventing it.

Julio Cortázar boasted in his later years that he was writing "worse all the time." He meant that in order to express what he longed to express in his stories and novels he was increasingly obliged to search out forms of expression further and further from classic forms, to defy the flow of language and try to impose upon it rhythms, patterns, vocabularies, and distortions in such a way that his prose might more convincingly represent the characters or occurrences he invented. In truth, Cortázar's bad writing was very good writing. His prose was clear and fluid, beautifully imitating speech, incorporating and assimilating with perfect assurance the flourishes, quirks, and phrasings of the spoken word: he made use of Argentine colloquialisms, of course, but also French turns of phrase, and he invented words and expressions with such ingenuity and such a good ear that they didn't stand out in his sentences but rather enriched them with the "leavening" that Azorín believed was required of a good novelist.

The credibility of a story (its power to persuade) doesn't depend solely on the coherence of the style in which it is told—no less important is the role played by narrative technique. But without coherence there is no credibility, or it is reduced almost to nil.

A writer's style may be unpleasant and yet, thanks to its coherence, effective. Such is the case of someone like Louis-

Ferdinand Céline, for example. You may not agree with me, but I find irritating his short, stuttering little sentences, plagued with ellipses and packed with exclamations and slangy expressions. And yet I have no doubt that *Journey to the End of the Night* and also, though not so unequivocally, *Death on the Installment Plan* are novels possessed of an overwhelming power of persuasion. Their sordid outpourings and extravagance hypnotize us, making irrelevant any aesthetic or ethical objections we in good conscience might raise.

I have a similar reaction to the Cuban writer Alejo Carpentier, without a doubt one of the greatest novelists of the Spanish language. Taken out of the context of his novels, his prose is exactly the opposite of the kind of writing I admire (I know it's impossible to make such a distinction, but I make it to clarify my point). I don't like his stiffness, his academicism, and his bookish mannerisms, which always give me the sense that they are informed by meticulous searches in dictionaries, a product of that old passion for archaisms and artifice that seized the Baroque writers of the seventeenth century. And yet this same prose, when it tells the story of Ti Noel and Henri Christophe in Carpentier's 1949 novel *The Kingdom of This World*, an absolute masterwork that I've read at least three times, cancels out my reservations and antipathies with its contagious and overwhelming power and dazzles me, making me believe wholeheartedly everything it has to tell. How does the starched and buttoned-up style of Alejo Carpentier accomplish such a thing? Through its unflagging coherence and its aura of indispensability. His style has about it a conviction that makes its readers feel that he tells the story the only way it could be told: in *these* words, phrases, and rhythms.

It is relatively easy to speak of the coherence of a style and harder to explain what I mean by *essentiality*, a quality required of the language of a novel if that novel is to be persuasive. Maybe the best way of describing essentiality is to explain its opposite, the style that fails in telling a story because it keeps us at a distance and lucidly conscious; in other words, a style that makes us conscious of reading something alien and prevents us from experiencing the story alongside its characters and sharing it with them. This failure is perceived when the reader feels an abyss that the novelist does not successfully bridge in writing his tale, an abyss between what is being told and the language in which it is told. This bifurcation or split between the language of a story and the story itself annihilates the story's power of persuasion. The reader doesn't believe what he is being told, because the clumsiness and inconvenience of the style make him sense that between word and deed there is an unbreachable divide, a fissure that exposes all the artifice and arbitrariness that fiction depends on and that only successful fictions manage to erase or hide.

Such a style fails because we don't feel it is necessary; indeed, as we read we realize that the same story told in a different way or in other words would be better (which in literary terms simply means more persuasive). We never feel any dichotomy of language and content when we read Faulkner's novels or the stories of Borges or Isak Dinesen. The styles of these authors—each so very different—persuade us because in them words, characters, and things constitute an indissoluble unity; it is impossible to conceive of the parts in isolation. It is this perfect integration of style and content that I am alluding to when I speak of the quality of *essentiality* any creative writing must possess.

The *essentiality* of the language of great writers is detected, by contrast, in the forced and false writing of their epigones. Borges is one of the most original prose stylists of the Spanish language, and perhaps the greatest Spanish stylist of the twentieth century. For that very reason, he has exerted a great influence and, if I may say so, an unfortunate one. Borges's style is unmistakable and functions extraordinarily well, giving life and credibility to a world of sophisticated intellectual and abstract ideas and curiosities. In this world, philosophical systems, theological disquisitions, myths and literary symbols, reflection and speculation, and universal history (contemplated from an eminently literary perspective) are the raw material of invention. Borges's style adapts itself to its subject matter and merges with it in a powerful alloy, and the reader feels from the first sentences of his stories and of many of his essays that these works have the inventive and sovereign quality of true fictions, that they could only have been told in this way, in this intelligent, ironic, and mathematically precise language—not a word too few, not a word too many—with its cold elegance and aristocratic defiance, privileging intellect and knowledge over sensation and emotion, playing with erudition, making a technique of presumption, eluding all forms of sentimentality, and ignoring the body and sensuality (or noting them at a great distance, as lower manifestations of existence). His stories are humanized thanks to their subtle irony, a fresh breeze that lightens the complexity of the arguments, intellectual labyrinths, and baroque constructions that are almost always their subject matter. The color and grace of Borges's style lies first and foremost in his use of adjectives, which shake the reader with their audacity and eccentricity ("No one saw him disembark in the *unanimous* night"), and in his violent and unexpected metaphors, whose adjectives and adverbs, besides fleshing out an idea or highlighting a physical or psychological trait, often serve to foster a Borgesian atmosphere. Precisely because it is essential, Borges's style is inimitable. When his admirers or literary followers copy his way of using adjectives, his irreverent sallies, his witticisms and poses, their stylings are as out of place as badly made wigs that fail to pass as real hair, proclaiming their falseness and bringing ridicule down on the unhappy heads they cover. Jorge Luis Borges was a formidable creator, and there is nothing more irritating or bothersome than the "mini-Borges" imitators whose imitations lack the essentiality of the prose they mimic, making what was original, authentic, beautiful, and stimulating something caricaturish, ugly, and insincere. (The question of sincerity or lack of sincerity in literature is not an ethical issue but an aesthetic one.)

Something similar has happened around another great prose stylist, Gabriel García Márquez. Unlike Borges's style, his is not sober but exuberant and not intellectualized at all; rather, it is sensory and sensual. Its clarity and correctness reveal its classical origins, but it is not stiff or old-fashioned—it is open to the assimilation of sayings and popular expressions and to neologisms and foreign words, and it possesses a rich musicality and conceptual purity free of complications or intellectual wordplay. Heat, taste, music, all the textures of perception and the appetites of the body are expressed naturally and without fuss, and fantasy draws breath with the same freedom, casting itself unfettered toward the extraordinary. Reading *One Hundred Years of Solitude* or *Love in the Time of Cholera* we are overwhelmed by the certainty that only in these words, with this grace and rhythm, would these stories be believable, convincing, fascinating, moving; that separated from these words they would not have been able to enchant us as they have: his stories *are* the words in which they are told.

And the truth is that words are also the stories they tell. As a result, when a writer borrows a style, the literature that is produced sounds false, like mere parody. After Borges, García Márquez is the most imitated writer in the language, and although some of his disciples have been successful—that is to say, they've attracted many readers—the work, no matter how diligent the disciple, fails to take on a life of its own, and its secondary, forced character is immediately evident. Literature is pure artifice, but great literature is able to hide the fact while mediocre literature gives itself away.

Although it seems to me that now I've told you everything I know about style, in view of your letter's demands for *practical* advice, I'll give you this: since you want to be a novelist and you can't be one without a coherent and essential style, set out to find a style for yourself. Read constantly, because it is impossible to acquire a rich, full sense of language without reading plenty of good literature, and try as hard as you can, though this is not quite so easy, not to imitate the styles of the novelists you most admire and who first taught you to love literature. Imitate them in everything else: in their dedication, in their discipline, in their habits; if you feel it is right, make their convictions yours. But try to avoid the mechanical reproduction of the patterns and rhythms of their writing, since if you don't manage to develop a personal style that suits your subject matter, your stories will likely never achieve the power of persuasion that makes them come to life.

It is possible to seek out and find a style of your own. Read Faulkner's early novels. You'll see that from the mediocre *Mosquitoes* to the estimable *Flags in the Dust*, as the first version of *Sartoris* was called, Faulkner found *his* style, the labyrinthine and majestic language, part religious, part mythical, and part epic, that animates the Yoknapatawpha novels. Flaubert also sought and found his style between the first version of *The Temptation of Saint Anthony*, written in a torrential, unmoored, lyrically romantic fashion, and *Madame Bovary*, in which that unbridled style was severely curtailed and all the emotional and lyrical exuberance in it sternly repressed in favor of an "illusion of reality," which he managed to perfect in five years of superhuman labor, the same amount of time it took him to compose his first masterpiece. As you may know, Flaubert had a theory about style, that of the mot juste. The right word was the one word—the only word—that was able to express an idea aptly. The obligation of the writer was to find that word. How did he know when he had? A whisper in his ear: the word was right when it *sounded* right. The perfect correspondence between form and content—between word and idea—translated itself into musical harmony. That is why Flaubert submitted his sentences to *"la gueulade,"* the shouting test. He'd go outside to read aloud everything he had written, out to an avenue of lime trees that still exists near what used to be his house at Croisset: the *"allée des gueulades,"* the shouting allée. There he'd read as loudly as he could what he'd written, and his ear would tell him if he'd succeeded or if he'd have to keep trying out words and sentences until he achieved the artistic perfection he pursued with such fanatic tenacity.

Do you remember the line by Rubén Darío "My style in search of a form"? For a long time, I was disconcerted by it: aren't style and form the same thing? How is it possible to search for form when it is there in front of you? Now I understand better because, as I mentioned in one of my earlier letters, writing is only one aspect of literary form. Another, no less important, is technique, since words alone do not suffice in the telling of good stories. But this letter has gone on too long, and I'd better leave that discussion for next time.

Fondly,

The Narrator and Narrative Space

DEAR FRIEND,

I'm glad you encourage me to discuss the structure of
the novel, the framework that sustains the fictions that dazzle us as harmonious and living entities, their persuasive
power so great they seem all-encompassing, self-generated,
and self-contained. But we already know that that is only
what they seem. Ultimately, it is not what they are: the magic
of their prose and the dexterity of their construction only
manage to give that illusion. We've already discussed narrative style. Now we must consider the ways in which the
elements of the novel are organized and the techniques the
novelist employs to invest his inventions with the power of
suggestion.

The variety of problems or challenges that those who set
out to write fiction must confront may be divided into four
major categories, as follows:

a. narrator
b. space

c. time

d. level of reality

That is to say, the ability of a story to surprise, move, uplift, or bore us depends as much upon the choice and handling of the narrator and three points of view, all closely interwoven, as upon the effectiveness of the story's style.

Today I'd like to discuss the narrator, the most important character in any novel and the one upon whom, in a way, all the rest depend. But first of all we must clear up a common misunderstanding: the narrator—that is, the person who tells the story—must not be confused with the author, the person who writes it. This is a very serious error, made even by many novelists who, having decided to tell their stories in the first person and deliberately taking their own biographies as their subject matter, believe that they are the narrators of their fictions. They are mistaken. A narrator is a being made of words and not of flesh and blood, as authors tend to be; the former lives only within the confines of the story that is being told, and only while he is telling it (the boundaries of the story are those of his existence). The author has a much richer and fuller life, which predates the writing of a particular novel and survives it. Even while he is writing a novel, it does not entirely occupy his existence.

The narrator is always a made-up character, a fictional being, just like all the other characters whose story he "tells," but he is the most important because the way he acts—showing or hiding himself, lingering or surging ahead, being explicit or elusive, talkative or taciturn, playful or serious—decides whether we will be persuaded of the reality of the other characters and whether we will be convinced that they are not puppets or caricatures. The behavior of the narrator establishes the internal coherence of a story, which, in turn, is an essential factor in determining its power to persuade.

The first problem the author must resolve is who will tell the story. The possibilities seem endless, but in general terms they may be reduced to three: a narrator-character, an omniscient narrator outside and separate from the story he tells, or an ambiguous narrator whose position is unclear—he may be narrating from either inside or outside the narrative world. The first two types of narrator are the most traditional; the last, on the other hand, has only very recently been established and is a product of the modern novel.

To determine which the author chose, one must just check which grammatical person the story is told in: whether it is a *he* or *she*, an *I*, or a *you*. The pronoun tells us what space the narrator occupies in relation to that of the story. If the narration is from the point of view of an *I* (or a *we*, a rare case, but not unheard of; remember *Citadelle* by Antoine de Saint-Exupéry or many passages in John Steinbeck's *The Grapes of Wrath*), the narrator is inside the narrative, interacting with the characters of the story. If the narrator speaks from the third-person singular, he is outside the narrative space and is, as in so many classic novels, an omniscient narrator modeled on an all-powerful God, since he sees everything—no matter how big or small—and knows everything but is not part of the world he proceeds to show us from the outside perspective of his soaring gaze. And what space is occupied by the narrator who narrates from the second-person *you*, as the narrator does, for example, in *Passing Time* by Michel Butor, *Aura* by Carlos Fuentes, *Juan the Landless* by Juan Goytisolo, *Five Hours with Mario* by Miguel Delibes, and many chapters of *Galíndez* by Manuel Vázquez Montalbán? There's no way of knowing beforehand; the answer may only be sought by examining the way the second person is employed. The *you* could be spoken by an omniscient narrator from outside the fictional world who goes about giving orders and commands and imposing his word as law, causing everything to happen in obedience to his will and the fully fledged, limitless powers he enjoys as an imitator of God. But the narrator might also be a consciousness turned inward and speaking to itself through the subterfuge of the *you*, a somewhat schizophrenic narrator-character who is involved in the novel's action but disguises his identity from the reader (and sometimes from himself) through the device of the split personality. In novels narrated by second-person narrators, there is no way to know for sure, and the answer must be deduced from internal narrative evidence.

The relationship that exists in all novels between the space the narrator occupies and the narrative space is called the *spatial point of view*, and we say that it is determined by the grammatical person in which the novel is narrated. The possibilities are three:

a. a narrator-character who narrates in the first-person singular, a point of view in which the space of the narrator and the narrative space coincide;

b. an omniscient narrator who narrates in the third person and occupies a space independent of and separate from the narrative space; and

c. an ambiguous narrator, concealed behind the second person, whose *you* might be the voice of an all-seeing and all-powerful narrator decreeing from outside the narrative space the course of fictional events or the voice of a narrator-character involved in the action who, whether timid or conniving or seized by schizophrenia or mere whim, reproduces himself and talks to himself as he addresses the reader.

Broken down in this way, I imagine the *spatial point of view* seems very clear, something identifiable by a simple glance at the first few sentences of a novel. That is true if we limit ourselves to abstract generalizations, but when we consider specific cases we discover that multiple variations fit within the scheme, permitting each author, having chosen a certain spatial point of view from which to tell his story, to avail himself of a wide range of innovations and variations, thereby assuring his originality and freedom.

Do you remember how *Don Quixote* begins? No doubt you do, since its first line is one of the most memorable in literature: "In a village of La Mancha the name of which I have no desire to recall . . ." Following our system of classification, we see that the narrator of the novel occupies the first-person singular, that he speaks as an *I*, and that he is therefore a narrator-character whose space is the same as the story's. Nevertheless, we soon discover that although this first-person narrator makes an appearance every so often (as in the first sentence) and speaks to us as *I*, he is not at all a narrator-character but rather an omniscient, God-like narrator who, from a lofty exterior perspective, narrates the action as if he were narrating from the outside, as a *he*. In fact, he does narrate as a *he*, except in a few instances in which he shifts to the first person and reveals himself to the reader, speaking from the perspective of an exhibitionistic and distracting *I* (since his sudden appearance in the middle of a story in which he plays no part is a gratuitous spectacle and distracts the reader from what is happening). These shifts or leaps in spatial point of view—from an *I* to a *he* and an omniscient narrator to a narrator-character or vice versa—alter the narrator's perspective or distance from the narrative and may or may not be justified. If they aren't justified—if the shifts in spatial perspective only serve as a self-congratulatory demonstration of the narrator's omnipotence—then the incongruity introduced conspires against illusion, weakening the persuasive power of the story.

But these shifts also give us an idea of the versatility a narrator may enjoy and the *transformations* he undergoes, modifying with his leaps from one grammatical person to another the perspective from which what is narrated unfolds.

Let's have a look at some interesting cases of versatility, of those spatial shifts or transformations of the narrator. Take the first sentence of *Moby-Dick*, "Call me Ishmael." Extraordinary beginning, isn't it? In just three words, Melville manages to awaken in us a lively curiosity regarding the mysterious narrator-character whose identity we can only guess at, since it's not even certain whether Ishmael is his name. The spatial point of view is certainly very well defined. Ishmael speaks in the first-person singular; he's a character in the story, though not the most important one—that role is reserved for the fanatical, possessed Captain Ahab or perhaps for his enemy, the maddening, ever-present absence that is the white whale he pursues—but he either witnesses or participates in most of the adventures he recounts (those he doesn't, he hears of secondhand and transmits to the reader). This point of view is rigorously respected by the author throughout the tale, but only until the final episode. Up until that point, the coherence of the spatial point of view is complete because Ishmael only tells (and only knows) what he is able to know as a person involved in the story, and this coherence strengthens the persuasive power of the novel. But in the end, as you'll recall, there comes the terrible moment when the fearsome sea beast becomes aware of Captain Ahab and the sailors on the *Pequod*. From an objective point of view, and to preserve the internal coherence of the story, the logical conclusion would be for Ishmael to succumb along with his companions. But if the logic of this development had been respected, how would it be possible for someone to be telling us a story when he dies at the end of it? To avoid this incongruity and to keep *Moby-Dick* from turning into a ghost story told by a narrator speaking from beyond the grave, Melville has Ishmael survive (miraculously) and informs us of his fate in a postscript to the tale. This postscript is not written by Ishmael himself but by an omniscient narrator, separate from the world of the narrative, an omniscient narrator who occupies a different, greater space than the narrative (since from it he can observe and describe the space in which the narrative unfolds).

I hardly need point out something you've surely already realized, which is that these shifts in narrator are not unusual. On the contrary, it is common for novels to be told (though we might not always notice it at first) not by one narrator but by two or sometimes several, who relieve each other every so often, like runners in a relay race.

The most obvious example of this narrative handing off—of spatial shifts—that occurs to me is *As I Lay Dying*, the novel in which Faulkner describes the Bundren family's trip across Mississippi to bury their mother, Addie Bundren, who wanted to be laid to rest in the place where she was born. The trip has biblical and epic qualities, since the cadaver begins to decompose under the merciless sun of the Deep South, but the family presses on undaunted in their journey, animated by the fanatical conviction that Faulkner's characters tend to possess. Do you remember how the novel is told, or, to be more precise, who tells it? Many narrators: all the members of the Bundren family and others as well. The story passes along through the consciousness of each of them, establishing peripatetic and multiple points of view. The narrator is, in all cases, a narrator-character, involved in the action and settled in the narrative space. But although in this sense the spatial point of view remains unchanged, the identity of the narrator changes as the narrative is transferred from one character to the next, so that in this novel—unlike in *Moby-Dick* or *Don Quixote*—the shift is not between one spatial point of view and another but between one character and another, and requires no exiting of the narrative space.

If these shifts are justified and lend the novel a denser and richer verisimilitude, they are invisible to the reader, who is caught up in the excitement and curiosity awakened in him by the story. On the other hand, if they don't work, the effect is the opposite: their artifice is laid bare, and they seem forced and arbitrary to us, straitjackets squeezing spontaneity and authenticity out of the story's characters. This is not the case with *Don Quixote* or *Moby-Dick*, of course.

And neither is it the case with the marvelous *Madame Bovary*, another cathedral of the novel genre, in which we also witness a fascinating spatial shift. Do you remember the beginning? "We were in class when the headmaster came in, followed by a new boy, not wearing the school uniform, and a school servant carrying a large desk." Who is the narrator? Who is speaking to us in the person of that *we*? We'll never know. All we know for sure is that it is a narrator-character whose space is the same as the narrative's space and who is a witness to what he is telling since he tells it in the first-person plural. Since the narrator is a *we*, the possibility cannot be discounted that it is a collective character, perhaps the group of students whose class the young Monsieur Bovary joins. (If you'll allow me to cite a pygmy alongside the giant Flaubert, I once wrote a novella, *The Cubs*, from the spatial point of view of a collective narrator-character, the group of neighborhood friends of the protagonist, Pichulita Cuéllar.) But it could also be a single student, who discreetly, modestly, or timidly speaks as "we." In any case, this point of view is maintained for only a few pages, over the course of which we hear that first-person voice relating an episode two or three times and presenting himself or herself unequivocally as a witness to it. But at a moment difficult to define—the subtlety is evidence of another technical feat—the voice ceases to be that of a narrator-character and shifts to that of an omniscient narrator, distant from the tale, located in a different space, who no longer narrates as *we* but in the third-person singular, as *he*. The shift is from one point of view to another: in the beginning, the voice is that of a character, and then it becomes that of an omniscient and invisible God, who knows all and sees all and tells all without revealing or describing himself or herself. This new point of view is rigorously sustained until the end of the novel.

Flaubert, who developed a whole theory of the novel in his letters, was an unflagging champion of the invisibility of the narrator, since he maintained that what we have termed the autonomy or self-sufficiency of a fiction requires the reader to forget that what he's reading is being narrated; he must be under the impression that it is coming to life in the act, as if generated by something inherent in the novel itself. To create an invisible omniscient narrator, Flaubert invented and perfected many techniques, the first of which was an adherence to the neutrality and impassibility of the narrator. Commentary, interpretation, and judgment represent intrusions of the narrator into the story and are signs of a presence (in space and reality) different from the presences that make up the reality of the novel; the intrusion of the narrator destroys the illusion of self-sufficiency, betrays the accidental, derivative nature of the story, and shows it to be dependent on something or someone external to itself. Flaubert's theory of the "objectivity" of the narrator—objectivity being the price paid for invisibility—has long been followed by modern-day novelists (though often they do not realize it) and that is why it is perhaps no exaggeration to call Flaubert the first writer of the modern novel, tracing between it and the romantic or classical novel a technical divide.

That is not to say, of course, that because the narrators of romantic or classical novels are less invisible and sometimes all too visible, those novels seem defective or awkward to us or lacking in power of persuasion. Not at all. It means that when we read a novel by Dickens, Victor Hugo, Voltaire, Daniel Defoe, or Thackeray, we must resituate ourselves as readers, adapt ourselves to a different spectacle from the one we're used to in the modern novel.

This difference has to do especially with the different ways in which an omniscient narrator manifests himself in modern novels and in novels that we call romantic or classical. In the former, he tends to be invisible, or at least discreet, and in the latter, a distinct presence, sometimes so overbearing that as he narrates he seems to tell his own story and sometimes even takes what he is telling us as a pretext for unbridled exhibitionism.

Isn't that what happens in *Les Misérables*? One of the most ambitious narrative creations of the nineteenth century—the golden age of the novel—*Les Misérables* is steeped in all the great social, cultural, and political events of its time and in all of Victor Hugo's personal experiences over the nearly thirty years he spent writing it (he returned to the manuscript several times after abandoning it for long intervals). It is no exaggeration to say that the novel includes a formidable display of exhibitionism and egomania on the part of its narrator. The narrator is omniscient, technically separate from the world of the narrative, observing from outside the space where the lives of Jean Valjean, Monseigneur Bienvenu, Gavroche, Marius, Cosette, and the other abundant human fauna of the novel intersect. But in truth, the narrator is more present in the tale than the characters themselves: possessed of a proud and overbearing nature and seized by an irresistible megalomania, he can't keep from constantly revealing himself as he presents the story to us. Often he interrupts the action, shifts into the first-person singular from the third to weigh in on whatever he likes, pontificates on philosophy, history, morality, and religion, and judges his characters, mercilessly condemning them or praising them to the heavens for their civic-minded and spiritual inclinations. This narrator-God (and the epithet was never better employed) not only gives us constant proof of his existence and of the lesser and dependent status of the narrative world but also reveals to us—besides his convictions and theories—his phobias and sympathies, proceeding without the slightest discretion or precaution or scruple, convinced of the truth and justice of everything he thinks, says, or does in the name of his cause. In the hands of a less skillful and powerful novelist than Victor Hugo, these intrusions would entirely destroy the novel's power to persuade. The intrusions of an omniscient narrator constitute what contemporary critics call a "rupture of the system," a series of incursions introducing incoherencies and incongruencies liable to vanquish all illusion and strip the story of credibility in the reader's eyes. But that's not what happens in *Les Misérables*. Why not? Because the modern reader rapidly becomes accustomed to the intrusions and feels them to be an intrinsic part of the narrative system, of a fiction that is really two stories intimately intertwined and inextricably bound up together: the narrative that begins with Jean Valjean's theft of silver from the home of the bishop Monseigneur Bienvenu and concludes forty years later when the ex-convict, redeemed by the sacrifices and virtuous deeds of his heroic life, steps into eternity; and the story of the narrator, whose embellishments, exclamations, reflections, judgments, whims, and sermons constitute the intellectual context, an ideological-philosophical-moral backdrop to the text.

Might we, in imitation of the egocentric and impulsive narrator of *Les Misérables*, pause here to summarize what has been said about the narrator, the spatial point of view, and the space of the novel? I don't think the digression is unwarranted, because if everything has not been made clear I'm afraid that what I have to say next, encouraged by your interest, commentary, and questions, will seem confusing and even incomprehensible—and it's hard to make me stop in the middle of any discussion of the fascinating form of the novel.

In order to tell a story in writing, all novelists invent a narrator—their fictional representative or agent—who is as much a fiction as the other characters whose story he tells, since he is made of words and only lives for and as part of the novel he inhabits. This character, the narrator, may be situated inside the story, outside it, or in an uncertain location, depending on whether he narrates in the first, third, or second person. The choice is not random: the narrator's distance from and knowledge of the story he is telling will vary depending on the space he occupies relative to the novel. It is obvious that a narrator-character cannot know—and therefore, cannot describe or relate—matters other than those credibly within his reach, while an omniscient narrator can know everything and be everywhere in the narrative world. Whichever point of view is chosen, therefore, it is accompanied by a set of conditions, and if the narrator fails to abide by those conditions, the novel's power to persuade is impaired. Conversely, the closer the narrator keeps to the limits the spatial point of view imposes, the stronger the power of persuasion and the more real the narrative will seem to us, imbued with the "truth" that all great lies passing as good novels seem to possess.

It must be stressed that the novelist enjoys absolute freedom when he sets out to create his narrator. In other words, the distinction between the three possible types of narrator does not in any way indicate that their spatial placement limits their attributes or personalities. In a few examples we've seen how omniscient narrators—the all-seeing, God-like narrators of a Flaubert or a Victor Hugo—differ from one another, never mind narrator-characters, who are as infinitely variable as fictional characters in general.

We've also seen something that should perhaps have been mentioned explicitly from the start, something that for the sake of expository clarity I didn't bring up but that you likely already know, or have discovered reading this letter, since it is evident in the examples cited. Namely: it is rare and almost impossible for a novel to have only one narrator. Most common is that it should have many, a series of narrators who take turns telling the story from different perspectives, sometimes from the same spatial point of view (that of a narrator-character, in books like *La Celestina* or *As I Lay Dying*, which function like stage plays), sometimes from shifting ones, as in the examples from Cervantes, Flaubert, or Melville.

We can push our analysis of the spatial point of view and the spatial shifts of narrators a little further still. If we move in with a magnifying glass and make a meticulous freeze-frame examination (this is a terrible and unacceptable way to read a novel, of course), we discover that shifts take place not only in a general manner and over long stretches of narrative time as in the examples I've used. They can be swift and very brief, lasting barely a few words, in which the narrator undergoes a subtle and inconspicuous spatial shifting.

For example, whenever dialogue between characters lacks formal attribution, there is a spatial shift, a change of speaker. If, in a novel featuring Pedro and María and narrated by an omniscient narrator outside the story, this exchange is suddenly inserted:

"I love you, María."

"I love you too, Pedro."

then in the very brief instant in which Pedro and María declare their love for each other there is a shift: the narrator ceases to be omniscient and becomes a narrator-character involved in the narrative (Pedro and María), and within the spatial point of view of the narrator-character there is another shift between the two characters (from Pedro to María), after which the story returns to the spatial point of view of the omniscient narrator. Naturally, these shifts would not have occurred if that brief dialogue had been formally attributed ("I love you, María," *said Pedro.* "I love you too, Pedro," *replied María*), since then the story would have been consistently narrated from the point of view of the omniscient narrator.

Do these infinitesimal shifts, so rapid that the reader doesn't even notice them, seem insignificant to you? They are not. In fact, nothing is without importance in the formal domain, and it is the sum of these tiny details that decides the excellence or lack of merit of a work of art. What is evident, in any event, is that the author's unlimited freedom in creating and manipulating his narrator (moving him, hiding him, exhibiting him, bringing him into the foreground, pushing him into the background, turning him into different narrators or multiple narrators within a single spatial point of view, or leaping between different spaces) is not, nor can it ever be, arbitrary, but must find its justification in the novel's power of persuasion. The shifts in point of view can enrich a story, give it depth, give it subtlety, make it mysterious, ambiguous, multifaceted; or they can smother and crush it if instead of causing events to multiply of their own accord in an illusion of life these displays of technique—mechanical tricks in this case—give rise to incongruities and gratuitous complications or confusions that destroy the story's credibility and make evident to the reader its origins as mere artifice.

I'll hear from you soon I hope.

Fondly,

Time

I'm glad that these reflections on the structure of the novel are yielding you a few clues, pointing you the way into the depths of fiction as if you were a spelunker venturing deep into the heart of a mountain. Now that we've touched on the characteristics of the narrator in relation to the space of the novel (which in disagreeably academic language I termed the *spatial point of view*), I propose that we examine time, a no less important aspect of narrative form, the treatment of which is as crucial as the treatment of space in determining the persuasive power of a story.

On this subject we must also first dispel some prejudices, venerable yet false, in order to understand what a novel is and how it works.

I refer to the naive equation that is often made between real time (to be called, redundant though the definition may be, the chronological time we readers and authors inhabit) and fictional time, a time or passage of time as imaginary as the narrator and characters trapped in it. As with the spatial point of view, huge doses of creativity and imagination go into the creation of the temporal point of view of all the novels we read, although in many cases their authors don't realize it. The time novels take place in is a fictional creation, just like the narrator and the setting; it is one of the elements the novelist manipulates to liberate his invention from the real world and give it the (apparent) autonomy upon which, I repeat, his power of persuasion depends.

Although the theme of time, a source of fascination for so many thinkers and creators (among them Borges, who made it the subject of many of his works), has given rise to a number of different and divergent theories, all of us, I think, can agree on at least one simple distinction: there are two kinds of time, chronological and psychological. The former exists objectively, independent of human subjectivity. It is in chronological time that we measure the movement of heavenly bodies in space and the positions the planets occupy with respect to one another; it is chronological time that eats away at us from the moment we are born until the moment we die and presides over the fateful life curve of all sentient beings. But there is also a psychological time, of which we are conscious depending on what we are doing or not doing and which figures very differently in our emotional lives. This time passes quickly when we are enjoying ourselves and when we are immersed in overwhelmingly intense, absorbing, or distracting experiences. On the other hand, it drags and seems infinite—the seconds like minutes, the minutes like hours—when we are waiting or suffering and our circumstances (loneliness, a long vigil, catastrophe, a wait for something that may or may not happen) give us a sharp awareness of the passing of time, which, precisely because we desire it to speed up, seems to sputter, slow, and stop.

I assure you that it is the rule (another of the very few binding rules in the world of fiction) that time in the novel is based not on chronological time but on psychological time, a subjective time to which the novelist (the *good* novelist) is able to give the appearance of objectivity, thereby setting the novel apart from the real world (which is the obligation of all fiction that desires to live of its own accord).

An example might make this clearer. Have you read the wonderful short story by Ambrose Bierce called "An Occurrence at Owl Creek Bridge"? It takes place during the American Civil War. Peyton Farquhar, a southern planter who has tried to blow up a rail line, is about to be hanged from a bridge. The story begins as the rope tightens around the poor man's neck; he is surrounded by the soldiers in charge of his execution. But when the order that will end his life is given, the rope breaks and the condemned man falls into the river. Somehow he manages to swim to shore and dodge the bullets of the soldiers on the bridge and the banks of the river. The omniscient narration is nearly at one with Peyton Farquhar's consciousness as he flees through the woods toward the safety of his home and the woman he loves, recalling episodes from his past as he runs with the soldiers at his heels. The narrative is harrowing, as is Farquhar's perilous flight. The house is there, within sight, and when the fugitive crosses the threshold, he at last glimpses his wife's profile. Just as he is about to embrace her, he is choked by the rope that had begun to tighten around his neck at the beginning of the story one or two seconds before. All of this occurs in the briefest flash; it is an instant, fleeting vision prolonged by the narrative, which creates its own separate time composed of words and different from real time (the objective time of the story's action, of which barely a second elapses). Doesn't this example make clear the way in which fiction constructs its *own* time out of psychological time?

A variation on this theme is a famous story by Borges, "The Secret Miracle." At the moment a Czech poet named Jaromir Hladik is about to be executed, God grants him another year of life, allowing him to complete—mentally— the drama in verse he had been planning to write all his life, *The Enemies*. Over the course of this year he successfully completes his ambitious work in the intimacy of his own mind, but the year he experiences is squeezed in between the order of "Fire" given by the head of the firing squad and the impact of the bullets as they riddle their target; that is to say, it lasts barely a fraction of a second, a mere instant. All fictions (and especially good ones) occupy their own time, a temporal system exclusively their own, different from the real time their readers inhabit.

To identify the basic characteristics of novelistic time, the first step is to divine the *temporal point of view* of the novel in question, which should never be confused with the spatial point of view, although in practice the two are viscerally linked.

There being no way to escape definitions (I'm sure they vex you as much as they do me, since they seem alien to the unpredictable world of literature), let's venture this one: the *temporal point of view* is the relationship that exists in all novels between the time the narrator inhabits and the time of what is being narrated. As with the spatial point of view, the novelist has only three to choose among (although the variations are many), and they are determined by the tense in which the narrator tells the story:

a. The time the narrator inhabits and the time of what is being narrated may coincide and be one and the same. In this case, the narrator narrates in the present tense.

b. The narrator may situate himself in the past to narrate events taking place in the present and the future. And, finally,

c. The narrator may situate himself in the present or the future and narrate events that have taken place in the (near or middle) past.

Although in their abstract form these distinctions may seem a little complicated, in practice they are quite obvious and easy to spot once we stop to check what tense the narrator has chosen to tell the story from.

Let's take as an example not a novel but a story, perhaps the shortest (and one of the best) in the world. "The Dinosaur," by Guatemalan writer Augusto Monterroso, is one sentence long:

"When he woke up, the dinosaur was still there."

A perfect story, is it not? Unbeatable power of persuasion, remarkable concision, perfect drama, color, suggestiveness, and clarity. Suppressing in ourselves all the very rich *other* possible readings of this minimalist narrative gem, let's concentrate on its temporal point of view. In what tense is it narrated? In a simple past tense: "he woke up." The narrator is situated, then, in the future, narrating something that happened—when? In the near or middle past from the narrator's future point of view? In the middle past. How do I know that the time of the story is a middle and not a near past in relation to the time of the narrator? Because between those two times there is an unbridgeable abyss, a gap, a barrier that abolishes all link or continuity between the two. This is the determining characteristic of the tense the narrator employs: the action is confined to a closed-off past, split from the time the narrator inhabits. The action of "The Dinosaur" takes place, therefore, in a middle past with respect to the time of the narrator; this is an example of case c.

Let us avail ourselves of "The Dinosaur" again to illustrate case a, the simplest and most obvious of the three: in it, the time of the narrator and the time of what is narrated coincide. This temporal point of view requires that the narrator narrate from the present tense:

"He wakes up and the dinosaur is still there."

The narrator and what is being narrated inhabit the same temporal space. The story is *happening* as the narrator tells it to us. This tale is very different from the previous one, in which we noted two tenses and in which the narrator, because he was situated in a later time than that of the narrative events, had a full-fledged and complete temporal vision of what he was narrating. In case a, the knowledge or perspective of the narrator is narrower: it only covers what is happening as it is happening; that is to say, as it is being told. When the time of the narrator and the time of the narrative are confused in a present tense (as is usually true in novels by Samuel Beckett or Alain Robbe-Grillet), the immediacy of the narrative is maximized; immediacy is minimal when the narrator narrates in the past tense.

Let's examine case b now, the least common and certainly the most complex: the narrator is situated in the past and narrates events that haven't taken place yet but will take place in a near or middle future. Here are examples of possible modes of this *temporal point of view*:

a. "You'll wake up, and the dinosaur will still be there."
b. "When you wake up, the dinosaur will still be there."
c. "When you have woken up, the dinosaur will still be there."

Each case (others are possible) constitutes a slight shading, establishing a different distance between the time of the narrator and the time of the narrated world, but the common denominator is that the narrator is narrating events that haven't taken place yet, that will take place when he has finished narrating them, and over which, as a result, an essential indeterminacy hovers: there is no certainty that they *will occur*, as there is when the narrator locates himself in a present or future tense to narrate events that have already occurred or that are occurring as they are narrated. Besides shading his story with relativity and uncertainty, the narrator located in the past who narrates events that will occur in a middle or near future reveals himself more aggressively, exhibiting his God-like powers in the fictional universe. Through the use of future tenses, his story becomes a series of imperatives, a sequence of orders commanding that what is being narrated must occur. The dominance of the narrator is absolute and overwhelming when a fiction is narrated from this *temporal point of view*. Hence a novelist can't use it without being conscious of it; he can't use it if he doesn't mean to manipulate uncertainty and allow the narrator a show of force in order to tell something that *only told in this way* will achieve power of persuasion.

Once the three possible temporal points of view have been identified, along with the variations permitted by each, and once we have established that the way to decide which point of view is being used is to check the tense that the narrator narrates from and the tense the story is narrated in, it is necessary to add that it would be very strange if a story were told from only one *temporal point of view*. Although in general one point of view dominates, the narrator usually moves from one *temporal point of view* to another, in shifts (changes of tense) that are more effective the less they call attention to themselves. This effectiveness is achieved by ensuring the coherence of the temporal system (the shifts in time must keep within certain boundaries) and the essentiality of the shifts, which should not seem whimsical or flashy but rather should lend an extra dimension—density, complexity, diversity, depth—to the characters and the story.

Without getting too technical, we may say, above all when speaking of modern novels, that a story flows in time just as it does in space, since novelistic time is something that stretches, lags, freezes, or suddenly speeds precipitously ahead. The story moves in fictional time as if in a physical territory, coming and going across it, moving forward in leaps and bounds or at a shuffle, leaving blank (wiping out) big chronological periods and going back later to pick up the thread of that lost time, leaping from the past to the future and back to the past with a freedom denied beings of flesh and blood in real life. This fictional time is therefore a creation just like the narrator.

Let's take a look at some examples of original constructions (or more obviously original constructions, I should say, since all are original) of fictional time. Instead of moving from the past to the present and then back to the future, the Alejo Carpentier story "Journey to the Seed" proceeds in the exact opposite direction: at the beginning of the story, Carpentier's protagonist, Don Marcial, the Marqués of Capellanías, is a dying old man and we watch him slip through maturity, youth, and childhood and finally retreat into a world of pure, unconscious sensation ("sensorial and tactile") where the character has yet to be born; he is still a fetus in the womb. The story isn't being told backwards; in this fictional world, time moves backwards. And, speaking of prenatal states, perhaps we should make reference to Laurence Sterne's *Tristram Shandy*, the first several dozen pages of which relate the prebirth biography of the narrator-protagonist, including ironic details about his complicated conception, his development in his mother's womb, and his arrival in the world. The twists, turns, spirals, and contortions of the tale make *Tristram Shandy*'s temporal structure a very odd and elaborate creation.

The coexistence in fiction of two or more tenses or temporal systems is also common. For example, in Günter Grass's *The Tin Drum*, time passes normally for everyone except the protagonist, the renowned Oskar Matzerath (he of the glass-shattering voice and the drum), who decides not to age, to abolish time. He succeeds, since by sheer force of will he stops growing and lives a kind of eternal life in a world that ages, perishes, and renews itself all around him, subjected to the inevitable decay imposed by the god Chronos. Everything and everyone fades away, except Oskar.

The theme of the abolition of time and its consequences (disastrous, according to fictional testimony) is a recurring one in fiction. It appears, for example, in a not very successful novel by Simone de Beauvoir, *All Men Are Mortal*. Julio Cortázar, playing a technical trick, engineered his best-known novel to explode the inexorable law of expiration that all living things must obey. The reader who reads *Hopscotch* following the rules suggested by the narrator in the Table of Instructions will *never* finish reading it, since the last two chapters refer endlessly back to each other, and in theory (not in practice, of course) the obedient and disciplined reader must spend the rest of his life reading and rereading those chapters, trapped in a temporal labyrinth with no hope of escape.

Borges liked to quote from *The Time Machine* by H. G. Wells (an author who was also fascinated by the theme of time), in which a man travels to the future and returns with a rose in his hand as proof of his adventure. This impossible displaced rose impressed Borges as a paradigm of the fantastic object.

Another case of parallel times is a story by Adolfo Bioy Casares, "The Celestial Plot," in which an aviator disappears in his plane and reappears later, telling an extraordinary tale that no one believes: he landed in a different time from the one he took off in. In his fictional universe many different parallel times mysteriously coexist, each with its own features, inhabitants, and rhythms, and the times never meet except in unusual instances like this pilot's accident, which reveals to us the structure of a universe that is like a pyramid of ascending temporal floors without connection to one another.

The opposite of these multiple temporal universes is a time so intensified by the narrative that the chronology and the passage of time slow down until they almost stop: as we recall, Joyce's huge novel *Ulysses* covers just twenty-four hours in the life of Leopold Bloom.

At this point in this long letter, you must be eager to interrupt me with an observation you are barely able to contain: "But in what you've written so far on the temporal point of view, I note a mix of different things: time as theme or plot (in the examples by Alejo Carpentier and Bioy Casares) and time as form, a narrative construction in which the plot unfolds (true of *Hopscotch* and its eternal time)." Fair enough. The only excuse I have (and it is relative, of course) is that I confused things on purpose. Why? Because I believe that it is precisely when you are examining the temporal point of view in fiction that you are best able to notice how inseparable "form" and "content" really are, though I've dissociated them in a brutal way to reveal the secret anatomy of the novel.

Time in all novels is, I repeat, a formal creation, since in fiction the story unfolds in a way it never could in real life; at the same time, the passing of fictional time, or the relationship between the time of the narrator and what is being narrated, depends entirely on the story's being told from a particular temporal perspective. This could be expressed the other way around, too: the story the novel tells *depends* on the temporal point of view. Actually, it all boils down to the same thing when we abandon the theoretical plane of our discussion and take a look at concrete novels. In them we discover that "form" does not exist (whether it is spatial or temporal or has to do with levels of reality) independently of the stories that give (or fail to give) the novels life and shape through the words in which they are told.

But let's move on and discuss something else that is common to all fictional narratives. In every story we note moments when time seems to be condensed, revealing its passage to the reader in a tremendously vivid way, seizing his or her full attention, and periods in which intensity flags and the vitality of the episodes lessens; distanced from us, these latter episodes fail to capture our attention and seem ordinary and predictable—they transmit information or commentary that is intended merely as filler and that serves only to link characters or events that would otherwise be left dangling. We may call the former episodes *cruxes* (*live time*, with a maximum concentration of occurrences), and the latter episodes *dead time*, or transition time. Nevertheless, it would be unfair to reproach a novelist for the existence of dead time, of episodes in his novels with nothing more than a linking function. They are useful too, since they establish continuity and create the illusion of a world, of beings immersed in a social setting, which novels must foster. Poetry may be an intensive genre, distilled to the essentials, without waste. The novel may not. Novels are long, unfolding over time (a self-created time), and they play at being "histories," following the path of their characters within a certain social context. This requires that the novel present *informative*, connective, inevitable subject matter, as well as the cruxes or episodes of maximum energy that propel the story (and that sometimes change its nature, swerving it into the future or the past, revealing in it unexpected depths or ambiguities).

The combination of cruxes or live time, and of dead or transition time, determines the configuration of time in the novel—that is, the particular chronological system of written stories, which may be broken down into three varieties of *temporal point of view*. But let me assure you that though what I've said about time has advanced us a little in our examination of the nature of fiction, there is still much to be discussed. That will become evident as we address other aspects of the novelistic enterprise. Because we are going to keep unwinding this interminable skein, are we not?

There you see, you've got me started, and now there's no stopping me.

Fondly, and until next time,

Levels of Reality

DEAR FRIEND,

I very much appreciate your quick response, and I'm pleased you want us to continue exploring the anatomy of the novel. It's good to know, too, that you don't have too many objections to my presentation of the spatial and temporal points of view.

I'm afraid, however, that the point of view we're about to explore won't be so easily explained, though it is just as important as the ones we've already discussed; we are venturing now into a much more nebulous realm than that of space or time. But let's not waste time on introductory remarks.

To begin with what is easiest—a general definition—let's say that the point of view in terms of level of reality is the relationship between the level, or plane, of reality on which the narrator situates himself to narrate the novel and the plane of reality on which the story takes place. As with space and time, the planes occupied by the narrator and by the story may coincide or they may be different, and it is their relationship that determines the kind of fiction that is produced.

I can imagine your first objection. "It may be easy to establish the three possible spatial points of view—the narrator within the narrative, outside of it, or in an uncertain location—and the temporal points of view, too, given the conventional division of time into present, past, and future, but aren't we faced with a boundless infinity when we consider reality?" That may be true. In theory, reality can be divided and subdivided into a boundless number of planes, giving rise to infinite points of view in fictional realities. But, my friend, don't let yourself be overwhelmed by that dizzying possibility. Fortunately, when we move from theory to practice (here, too, is an example of two sharply distinct planes), we find that fiction only really negotiates a limited number of levels and that, as a result, we may identify the most common expressions of the point of view in terms of level of reality (I don't like this formulation either, but I haven't been able to come up with anything better) without presuming to cover all of them.

Perhaps the most distinct and clearly opposed of the options are the "real" world and the "fantastic" world. (I use quotation marks to emphasize the relativity of these concepts, though without such terms we wouldn't be able to understand one another, and perhaps wouldn't even be able to use language.) I'm sure that although you may not like it much (I don't either), you'll agree that we should call real or realist (as opposed to fantastic) all persons, things, or occurrences that we are able to recognize and define through our own experience of the world, and call everything else fantastic. The notion of the fantastic, then, covers a whole range of levels: the magic, the miraculous, the legendary, the mythical, et cetera.

Now that we are provisionally in agreement, I can tell you that this juxtaposition of the real and the fantastic is one of the associations of opposed or identical planes that may occur in a novel between narrator and narrative. And to make it clearer for you, let's move on to a concrete example, making use once again of Augusto Monterroso's brief masterpiece "The Dinosaur."

"When he woke up, the dinosaur was still there."

What is the point of view in terms of level of reality in this story? You'll agree that *the narrative* is situated in the plane of the fantastic, since in the real world you and I inhabit it is improbable that prehistoric animals that appeared in our dreams—or in our nightmares—would turn up in an objective reality and that we would encounter them in the flesh at the foot of our beds when we opened our eyes. It's clear, then, that the level of reality of the narrative is an imaginary or fantastic reality. Is the narrator (omniscient and impersonal) situated on the same plane? I'd venture to say that he is not, that he establishes himself instead on a real or realist plane—in other words, one that is essentially opposite and contrary to that of the narrative. How do I know this? By the tiniest but most unmistakable of indications, a signal or hint that the careful narrator gives the reader as he tells his pared-down tale: the adverb *still*. The word doesn't just define an objective temporal circumstance indicating a miraculous occurrence (the passage of the dinosaur from a dreamworld to objective reality). It is also a call to attention, a display of surprise or astonishment at the remarkable event. Monterroso's *still* is flanked by invisible exclamation points and implicitly urges us to be surprised by the amazing thing that has happened. ("Notice, all of you, what is going on: the dinosaur is *still* there, when it's obvious that it shouldn't be, since in true reality things like this don't happen; they are only possible in a fantastic reality.") This is how we know the narrator is narrating from an objective reality; if he weren't, he wouldn't induce us through the knowing use of an amphibious adverb to take note of the transition of the dinosaur from dream to life, from the imaginary to the tangible.

I have here, therefore, the point of view in terms of level of reality of "The Dinosaur": it belongs to a narrator who, situated in a real world, relates a fantastic occurrence. Can you recall other, similar examples of this point of view? What happens, for example, in Henry James's long story, or short novel, *The Turn of the Screw*? Bly, the grim country house that serves as the setting of the tale, is haunted by ghosts, which appear to two poor children and their governess; it is the governess's testimony—transmitted to us by another narrator-character—that is the source of all the information we are given. As a result, there is no doubt that the story takes place—as far as theme and plot are concerned—on a fantastic plane. And on what plane is the narrator situated? Things begin to get a little complicated, as always with Henry James, who was a magician greatly skilled in the combination and manipulation of points of view, which means that his stories always radiate a subtle ambiguity and lend themselves to multiple interpretations. Remember that in the story there are *two* narrators, not one (or are there three, if we include the invisible and omniscient narrator who always precedes the narrator-character?). There is an unnamed primary or principal narrator who informs us that he has heard his friend Douglas read a story aloud written by the very governess who tells us the ghost story. That first narrator is plainly situated on a "real" or "realist" plane in order to relate the fantastic tale, which perplexes and amazes him as much as it does the reader. Then, too, it is clear that the other narrator, the second-level narrator, the governess who "sees" the ghosts, is not on the same plane of reality but inhabits a fantastic plane unlike the world we know from personal experience, where the dead return to earth to "grieve" in the houses they inhabited when they were alive and to torment the new inhabitants. So far we could say that this story's point of view in terms of level of reality involves a narration of fantastic events featuring two narrators, one situated on a realist or objective plane and the other—the governess—narrating from a fantastic perspective. But when we examine the story even more carefully, we perceive a new complication in this point of view. Most likely, the governess hasn't seen the famous ghosts but only believes she has seen them or has imagined them. If this interpretation is correct (in other words, if the reader chooses it as the correct interpretation)—and it has been advanced by a number of critics—it transforms *The Turn of the Screw* into a realist tale, though one narrated from a plane of pure subjectivity (that of hysteria or neurosis) of a repressed spinster who is probably naturally inclined to see things that are not and have never been part of the real world. The critics who propose this interpretation of *The Turn of the Screw* read it as realist fiction, since the real world also encompasses a subjective plane, home to visions, illusions, and fantasies. It is not the story's content but the subtlety of its telling that makes it seem fantastic; its point of view in terms of level of reality is the pure subjectivity of a psychologically unbalanced person who sees things that don't exist and mistakes her fears and fantasies for objective reality.

So we have here two examples of point of view in which there is a relationship between the real and the fantastic; this opposition is the kind of radical contradiction that characterizes the literary genre we call fantastic (into which we lump, I repeat, texts that differ quite significantly from one another). If we set out to examine this point of view in the writings of the most distinguished authors of fantastic literature of our time (Borges, Cortázar, Calvino, Rulfo, Pierre de Mandiargues, Kafka, García Márquez, Alejo Carpentier, to supply a quick list) we would discover that the matching up of these two separate universes—the real and the unreal or the fantastic, as they are embodied or represented by the narrator and the narrative—leads to an infinity of gradations and variations, to the point that it is perhaps not an exaggeration to say that the originality of a writer of fantastic literature depends above all on the way in which the point of view in terms of level of reality is manifested in his fiction.

Now, the opposition of planes that we have observed so far—the real and the unreal, the realist and the fantastic—is a fundamental opposition between different kinds of universes. But real or realist fiction also consists of separate planes—although each of them may exist and be recognizable to us through our objective experience of the world—and realist writers are able, as a result, to take advantage of many options regarding the level of reality in the fictions they invent.

Perhaps the most obvious discontinuity within the bounds of a realist universe is between the objective world—of things, events, and people existing in and of themselves—and the subjective, interior world of emotions, feelings, fantasies, dreams, and the psychological motivations of much behavior. If you make an effort, you will immediately be able to dredge up the names of a good many writers who fit—according to this arbitrary system of classification—into the category of objective writers, and others who may be called subjective writers, depending on whether their fictional worlds tend to be principally or exclusively situated on one or the other of those two sides of reality. Isn't it obvious that Hemingway would be grouped with the objectives and Faulkner with the subjectives? That Virginia Woolf figures among the latter and Graham Greene among the former? But I know, don't worry: we are in agreement that the objective-subjective dichotomy is too general and that writers grouped into either of these two broad, generic classes may be very different from one another. (And of course we agree that it is always the individual case that matters in literature, since generic models can never tell us what we would like to know about the particular nature of a certain novel.)

Let's take a look at some specific works, then. Have you read *Jealousy* by Alain Robbe-Grillet? I don't believe it's a masterpiece, but it is a very interesting novel, perhaps Robbe-Grillet's best, and one of the best produced by the movement that briefly caused a stir on the French literary scene in the sixties, *le nouveau roman*. Robbe-Grillet was its standard-bearer and theoretician; in his book of essays *For a New Novel*, he explains that his intention is to purge the novel of all psychologizing and, beyond that, of all subjectivity and introspection; he intends to focus on the exterior, physical surface of an objectivized world, whose reality resides in things that are "resistant, stubborn, present in the moment, irreducible." In adhering to this (very limiting) theory, Robbe-Grillet wrote some incredibly dull books, if you'll allow me the discourtesy, but also some texts whose un-deniable interest resides in what we might call his technical dexterity. For example, *Jealousy*. The title isn't very ob-jective—quite a paradox!—since in French it means both "window blind" and "jealousy," an amphibiology that disap-pears in Spanish [and English—*Tr.*]. The novel is, I'll venture to say, the description of an icy, objective stare, and the

anonymous and invisible human behind the stare is presum-
ably a jealous husband spying on his wife. The novelty (the
action, you might call it, if you were making a joke) of the
work isn't its plot, since nothing happens, or, more accu-
rately, nothing worth remembering happens; there is only
the tireless, distrustful, insomniac stare with which the
woman is besieged. She is entirely defined by the point of
view in terms of level of reality. It's a realist story (since
there's nothing in it that doesn't correspond to our experience of the world), told by a narrator outside the narrative
world but so close to the observer-character that we sometimes tend to confuse their voices. The novel keeps so rigorously to a single level of reality that the effect is sensory; the
narrative evokes a pair of reddened eyes that are always
observing, watching, missing nothing about the person they
are monitoring or her surroundings, and thus it can only
capture (and transmit) an exterior, sensory, physical, and
visual impression of the world, a world that is all surface—a
plastic reality—without emotional, psychological, or psychic
depth. This point of view is quite original. Of all the possible
planes or levels of reality, Robbe-Grillet confines himself to
one—the visual—to tell us a story that, for that very reason,
seems to take place exclusively on a plane of total objectivity.

It's clear that the plane or level of reality that Robbe-
Grillet's novels (especially *Jealousy*) inhabit is different from
that generally occupied by the works of Virginia Woolf,
another of the great revolutionaries of the modern novel.
Woolf wrote a fantastic novel, of course—*Orlando*—in which

we witness the impossible transformation of a man into a woman, but her other novels may be called realist, because they are lacking in similar marvels. Their "marvel" is the delicate and finely grained texture of the "reality" they portray. This is due to Woolf's refined and subtle style, its ethereal lightness, and its great power to suggest and evoke. On what plane of reality does one of her most original novels, *Mrs. Dalloway*, take place, for example? On that of human deeds and behavior, as in Hemingway's stories? No—on an interior and subjective plane, on the plane of feelings and emotions imprinted on the human spirit by life experience, in the intangible but demonstrable reality in which we register what takes place around us, what we see and do, and either rejoice in it or lament it, are moved or frustrated by it, and finally judge it. This level-of-reality point of view is another proof of Virginia Woolf's originality; she managed, thanks to her prose and the lovely, keen perspective from which she described her fictional world, to spiritualize all reality, dematerialize it, infuse it with soul. Exactly the opposite of a Robbe-Grillet, who developed a narrative technique with the aim of objectifying reality and described everything contained in it—including sentiments and emotions—as if they were things.

Through these few examples, I hope that you've come to the same conclusion I came to some time ago regarding point of view in terms of level of reality: that the originality of the novelist often resides in it. In other words, by uncovering (or throwing into relief, at least) one aspect or function of life or human experience previously overlooked, ignored, or suppressed in fiction and resurgent now as the dominant feature, the novelist grants us a pristine, refreshing, unfamiliar vision of life. Isn't this what happens in the work of a Proust or a Joyce? For the former, what is important is not what goes on in the real world but the way memory retains and reproduces lived experience, the way the human mind works to rescue and order the past; you couldn't ask for a more subjective reality than that in which the episodes and characters develop and evolve in *In Search of Lost Time*. And, speaking of Joyce, wasn't *Ulysses* a cataclysmic innovation? In it, reality is "represented" by the very motion of human consciousness as it notices, critiques, judges worthy, treasures or discards, and reacts emotionally and intellectually to the experiences lived through. By privileging planes or levels of reality once ignored or barely noted over more conventional planes, certain writers expand our understanding of human existence, not just quantitatively but in a qualitative sense too. Through writers like Virginia Woolf or Joyce or Kafka or Proust, we can say that our intellect has been enriched, as has our ability to identify—from within the infinite vertigo of planes or levels of reality—the mechanisms of memory, the absurd, the flow of consciousness, the subtleties of emotion and perception that we used to disregard and have a simplistic or stereotyped idea of.

All these examples demonstrate the very broad spectrum of shadings that may differentiate one realist author from another. The same is true of the writers of fantastic fiction, of course. Though this letter is in danger of running longer than it should, I'd like to examine the level of reality that predominates in *The Kingdom of This World* by Alejo Carpentier.

If we try to situate this novel in either the realist or the fantastic camp, there's no doubt that it should be assigned to the latter: in the story that Carpentier tells—which has much in common with the story of the real-life Haitian Henri Christophe, the builder of the celebrated Citadelle—extraordinary things take place, inconceivable in the world we know through firsthand experience. But no one who has read Carpentier's lovely tale will be content to see it classified simply as fantastic literature. Its fantastic passages are not as explicit and obvious as parts of stories by writers like Edgar Allan Poe, the Robert Louis Stevenson of *Dr. Jekyll and Mr. Hyde*, or Jorge Luis Borges, whose fiction flagrantly breaks with reality. In *The Kingdom of This World*, the unusual occurrences seem unusual because of their proximity to real life, to history—it so happens that the book very closely mirrors episodes and characters from Haitian history—and because they contaminate realist happenings. How can this be? It is possible because the narrative of Carpentier's novel is grounded in a plane of unreality associated with myth or legend; in this plane, "real" historical acts or characters undergo an "unreal" transformation when acted upon by faith or beliefs that give the fantastic text a kind of objective legitimacy. Myths explicate reality in terms of particular religious or philosophical convictions; all myths possess, besides their imaginary or fantastic element, an objective historical context. This determines their place in a subjective group consciousness that pretends to impose (and often succeeds in imposing) itself on reality, in the same way that a fantastic planet is superimposed on the real world by the members of a secret society in Borges's story "Tlön, Uqbar, Orbis Tertius." The incredible technical achievement of *The Kingdom of This World* is the point of view in terms of level of reality that Carpentier creates. The story often unfolds on a mythical or legendary plane—the first level of fantastic literature or the last of realism—and is narrated by an impersonal narrator who, though he doesn't establish himself entirely on that same level, comes very close to it, brushing up against it, so that the distance he maintains from his material is small enough to *almost* make us live inside the myths and legends of his story and yet unequivocal enough to make us realize that what we are being told is not objective reality but rather a reality undone by the credulity of a town that has not given up magic, witchcraft, or irrational practices, although on the outside it seems to have embraced the rationalism of the colonizers from whom it is emancipated.

We could go on forever trying to identify original and unusual points of view in the world of fiction, but I think that these examples are more than enough to show how various the relationship between the narrative and the narrator can be and how a discussion of levels of reality allows us to speak—if we're inclined to classify and catalog, which I'm not and I hope you're not either—of realist and fantastic novels, mythical and religious novels, psychological and lyrical novels, action-driven and analytical novels, philosophical and historical novels, surrealist and experimental novels, et cetera, et cetera. (The establishment of systems of classification is an insatiable vice.)

It's not important to know exactly where the novel we analyze fits on a series of pedantic and innumerable charts. What's important is to notice that in every novel there is a spatial point of view, a temporal point of view, and a level-of-reality point of view; to understand that the three are essentially independent of and different from one another, though their boundaries are often unclear; and to realize that the way the three points of view mesh and harmonize lends the novel the internal coherence that determines its power of persuasion. This ability to persuade us of "truth," "authenticity," and "sincerity" never comes from the novel's resemblance to or association with the real world we readers inhabit. It comes exclusively from the novel's own being, from the words in which it is written and from the writer's manipulation of space, time, and level of reality. If the words and the structure of a novel are efficient, and appropriate to the story that the novel intends to make persuasive, that means that its text is perfectly balanced. Theme, style, and points of view are so perfectly harmonized and the reader is so hypnotized and absorbed by what is being told that he completely forgets the *way* it is being told and is under the impression that technique and form have nothing to do with it, that life itself animates the work's characters, landscapes, and events, which seem to the reader nothing less than reality incarnate, life in print.

This is the great triumph of technical skill in novel writing: the achievement of invisibility, the ability to endow a story with color, drama, subtlety, beauty, and suggestive power so effectively that no reader even notices the story exists; under the spell of its craftsmanship, he feels that he is not reading but rather living a fiction that, for a while at least and as far as he is concerned, supplants life.

Fondly,

Shifts and Qualitative Leaps

DEAR FRIEND,

You're right: throughout our correspondence as we've discussed the three points of view that are common to all novels, I've used the expression *shifts* several times to refer to certain conversions a narrative undergoes, but I haven't really stopped to explain this common fictional device as carefully as I should. I'm going to describe the process now; it is one of the most ancient used by writers in the composition of their stories.

A "shift" is an alteration in any of the points of view we've examined. There may, therefore, be spatial shifts, temporal shifts, or shifts in level of reality. Frequently, especially in the twentieth century, novels have multiple narrators: sometimes various narrator-characters, as in Faulkner's *As I Lay Dying*, sometimes an omniscient, exterior narrator and one or more narrator-characters, as in Joyce's *Ulysses*. Each time, then, that the spatial perspective of the story changes—and it changes whenever there is a shift in narrator, which is evident when the grammatical person switches from *he* to *I*, from *I* to *he*, or otherwise fluctuates—a spatial shift is taking place. In some novels these shifts are frequent and in others they are rare, and only the end result indicates whether they are helpful or counterproductive and whether they reinforce or undermine the story's power of persuasion. When spatial shifts are effective, they manage to give a broad, variegated, even global and totalizing vision of a story (and thereby produce the illusion of independence from the real world that, as we've already noted, all fictional worlds secretly aspire to). If the shifts aren't effective, the result may be confusion: the reader is disoriented by the sudden and arbitrary leaps in perspective.

Perhaps less frequent than spatial shifts are temporal shifts, the movements of the narrator in time that cause a story to unfold simultaneously before our eyes in the past, present, or future. If the technique is well applied, they lend the story an illusion of chronological totality, of temporal self-sufficiency. There are writers who are obsessed with the subject of time—we've discussed a few—and that is evident not only in the subject matter of their novels but also in their construction of unusual and sometimes incredibly complex chronological systems. One example out of thousands: D. M. Thomas's novel *The White Hotel*, which was much discussed in its time. The novel tells the story of a terrible massacre of Jews in the Ukraine; the confessions that the protagonist, the singer Lisa Erdman, makes to her Viennese analyst, Sigmund Freud, are its slender backbone. From the temporal point of view, the novel is divided into three parts, which correspond to the past, present, and future of the chilling collective crime, the novel's crux. The temporal point of view shifts twice: from the past to the present (the massacre) and to the future of the narrative's central event. But this second shift, to the future, is not just temporal: it is also a shift in level of reality. The story, which until this moment had existed in a "realist," historical, objective plane, shifts after the massacre in the last chapter, "The Camp," into a fantastic reality, a purely imaginary plane, an ethereal, spiritual territory inhabited by beings shed of physical existence, shades or ghosts of the human victims of the slaughter. The temporal shift is also a qualitative leap, causing the narrative to change in nature. As a result of the shift, the story shoots from a realist world to a purely fantastic one. Something similar happens in Hermann Hesse's *Steppenwolf* when the immortal spirits of the great creators of the past appear to the narrator-character.

It is shifts in level of reality that give writers the best opportunity to organize their narrative materials in a complex and original fashion. In saying this I don't mean to denigrate shifts in space and time, where the possibilities are, for obvious reasons, more limited; I merely wish to emphasize that, given the existence of innumerable levels of reality, the possibility of shifts is correspondingly immense, and writers of all eras have learned to exploit this very versatile resource.

But before we venture deep into the rich terrain of shifts, it might perhaps be convenient to make a distinction. Shifts are defined, on the one hand, by the points of view in which they occur—spatial, temporal, or level of reality—and, on the other hand, by their supplementary or substantive (peripheral or essential) character. A mere temporal or spatial change is significant, but it doesn't entirely alter the substance of a story, whether the story is realist or fantastic. The kind of shift that occurs in a novel like *The White Hotel*, however, does change the nature of the tale, transferring it from an objective ("realist") world to a purely fantastic one. The shifts that provoke this ontological cataclysm—since they change the *being* of the narrative—may be called *qualitative leaps*, a term borrowed from the Hegelian dialectic; according to Hegel, quantitative accumulation triggers "a leap in quality" (like that of water, which becomes a gas when it boils long enough or is turned to ice when its temperature drops low enough). A narrative undergoes a similar transformation when a radical shift in the point of view in terms of level of reality occurs, constituting a *qualitative leap*.

Let's take a look at some striking examples from the rich arsenal of contemporary literature. In two contemporary novels published a good many years apart, for example, one Brazilian and the other English—*The Devil to Pay in the Backlands* by João Guimarães Rosa and *Orlando* by Virginia Woolf—the sudden change in sex of the main character (from man to woman in both cases) causes the entire narrative to undergo a qualitative shift, relocating the narrative from a plane that until that point seemed "realist" to one that is imaginary and even fantastic. In both instances, the shift is a crux, a central upheaval in the body of the narrative, an episode of maximum concentration of experiences that confers on its setting a quality it didn't seem to possess before. There is no such crux in Kafka's *Metamorphosis*, in which the remarkable event—poor Gregor Samsa's transformation into a horrible cockroach—takes place in the story's first sentence, positioning the story from the start in the realm of the fantastic.

These are examples of sudden and rapid shifts, abrupt acts that, because they are miraculous or extraordinary, skew the coordinates of the "real" world and give it a new dimension, a secret and marvelous configuration conforming not to rational or physical laws but rather to dark, fundamental forces that are only possible to understand (and, in some cases, control) through divine mediation, witchcraft, or magic. But in Kafka's most famous novels, *The Castle* and *The Trial*, the shift is a slow, involved, and stealthy process, the result of the accumulation or intensification in time of a certain state of things; in the end, the narrative world is emancipated from the objective reality—the "realism"—it pretended to imitate, and reveals itself as a different brand, a different species of reality. The mysterious Mr. K., the anonymous surveyor of *The Castle*, tries many times to reach the massive edifice that looms over the district where he has come to work and where he is the supreme authority. The obstacles he encounters are trivial at first; for a good stretch of the tale, the reader has the sense of being submerged in a tightly realist world, a world that appears to mirror the most ordinary, everyday aspects of reality. But as the story progresses and the unlucky Mr. K. seems more and more defenseless and vulnerable, confounded by obstacles that, we come to understand, aren't fortuitous or the by-product of a mere administrative inertia but the manifestations of a sinister secret mechanism that controls human actions and destroys individuals, we readers are seized with the consciousness—besides the mounting anguish we feel at the impotence in which humanity is mired in the story—that the novel's level of reality is not the objective and historical one familiar to us but another kind of reality, a symbolic and allegorical (or simply fantastic) imaginary version. (This, however, should not be taken to suggest that "fantastic" novels are any less capable of imparting illuminating lessons about human existence and our own reality.) The shift takes place, then, between two magnitudes or levels of reality much more slowly and tortuously than in *Orlando* or *The Devil to Pay in the Backlands*.

The same thing happens in *The Trial*, in which Mr. K. finds himself trapped in the nightmarish labyrinth of a political and judicial system that initially seems "realist" to us, a somewhat paranoid interpretation of the inefficiency and absurdities that lead to the excessive bureaucratization of justice. But then, as absurd occurrences become increasingly frequent and intense, at a certain moment we begin to realize that there is something more sinister and inhuman behind the administrative tangle that traps the protagonist and is gradually destroying him: an ominous system of a perhaps metaphysical nature in which a citizen's free will and ability to react vanish; a system that uses and abuses individuals like a puppet master manipulating puppets on a stage; an order that it is impossible to rebel against, one that is omnipotent, invisible, and deeply ingrained in human consciousness. Symbolic, metaphysical, or fantastic, this level of reality becomes evident gradually and progressively in *The Trial*, as in *The Castle*, so that it is impossible to determine the precise moment the metamorphosis takes place. The same is true of *Moby-Dick*, isn't it? The endless chase across the sea in pursuit of a white whale that, by virtue of its very absence, acquires an aura of evil legend and is seen as a mythical animal—doesn't it, too, undergo a shift or qualitative leap that transforms what was at first a realist novel into a tale classifiable as imaginary, symbolic, allegorical, metaphysical—or simply fantastic?

At this point, your head is probably full of memorable shifts and qualitative leaps from your favorite novels. And the truth is, writers from every age have made frequent use of the device, especially in fantastic fictions. Let's think back on some of the shifts that are still vivid in our memory, shifts that serve as reminders of the books we've enjoyed. I know! I'm sure I've guessed right: Comala! Isn't the name of that Mexican village the first that comes to mind when we think about shifts? And the association is an excellent one, since it's unlikely that anyone who has read Juan Rulfo's classic 1955 novel *Pedro Páramo* will ever forget the shock of discovering deep into the book that all the characters in the story are dead and that the fictional Comala is not part of "reality"— or not, at least, the reality the reader inhabits—but belongs to a literary reality, where the dead do not disappear but continue to live. This is one of the most effective shifts (of the radical, qualitative-leap kind) of contemporary Latin American literature. The way it is achieved is so masterful that if you set out to establish where it occurs in the space or time of the story, you're faced with a real dilemma. Because it is rooted in no precise episode, event, or moment but reveals itself little by little, gradually, insinuatingly, announcing its progress in vague signs and faint traces that we barely notice when we come across them. Only later, retroactively, do the string of clues and the accumulation of suspicious events and incongruities allow us to see that Comala is a town not of live beings but of ghosts.

But it might be a good idea to move on to other literary shifts less macabre than Rulfo's. The most engaging, exuberant, and amusing one I can think of takes place in the story "Letter to a Young Lady in Paris" by Julio Cortázar. An amazing shift in level of reality occurs when the narrator-character, the author of the letter in question, lets us know that he has the unfortunate habit of vomiting up bunnies. This is a serious qualitative leap in the middle of what is generally a lighthearted story, though there is a chance it ends in tragedy; the last sentences of the letter insinuate that the protagonist, overcome by the constant stream of bunnies, kills himself at the end of the tale.

This is a procedure Cortázar often employs in his stories and novels. He uses it essentially to unsettle things in his invented worlds, shifting from a fairly simple, everyday reality of predictable, banal, ordinary elements to another, fantastic world where extraordinary things happen, like humans vomiting bunnies, and in which there is often a hint of violence. You must have read "The Maenads," another of Cortázar's great stories, in which the narrative world undergoes a psychic transformation, this one progressive and exponential. At what first seems a harmless concert at the Corona Theater, the musicians' performance elicits the almost excessive enthusiasm of the audience; this enthusiasm degenerates into an explosion of savage, incomprehensible animal violence, a collective lynching or struggle to the death. At the end of this unexpected slaughter, we are discomfited and ask ourselves whether it all really happened or whether it was a horrible nightmare, an absurd occurrence taking place in "another world," a world governed by an unusual mix of fantasy, hidden terrors, and the darker impulses of the human spirit.

Cortázar knows how to use shifts better than almost any other writer, whether those shifts are gradual or sudden, and in space, time, or level of reality: in the unmistakable geography of his world, poetry and the imagination are linked with his infallible sense of what the surrealists called the incredible everyday, and the apparent simplicity and conversational ease of his clean, fluid prose, entirely free of mannerisms, disguise complex arguments and a great inventive audacity.

Now that we're recalling literary shifts that linger in memory, I must cite one (and it's a crux) that occurs in *Death on the Installment Plan* by Céline. I have no personal sympathy for Céline: his racism and anti-Semitism inspire repugnance in me; nevertheless, he wrote two great novels (the other is *Journey to the End of the Night*). In *Death on the Installment Plan*, there is an unforgettable episode in which the protagonist crosses the English Channel on a ferry full of passengers. The sea is rough, and the rocking of the little boat makes everyone on board — crew and passengers alike — seasick. And of course, in the kind of sordid and threatening atmosphere that so fascinated Céline, everybody starts to vomit. Up until this point, we are in a natural world — an incredibly vulgar and petty world, perhaps — but our feet are firmly planted in objective reality. However, the vomit that begins to fall on the reader, splashing him with all the filth and waste one can imagine Céline's organisms expelling, is so painstakingly and effectively described that the tale becomes detached from reality and turns into something nightmarish and apocalyptic, until finally it is not just a handful of seasick men and women but all the humans in the universe who seem to be coughing up their guts. As a result of this shift, the story changes levels of reality and moves into a visionary, symbolic, and even fantastic plane; everything in the narrative is affected by the extraordinary transformation.

We could keep on discussing shifts indefinitely but that would mean repeating ourselves, since the examples cited more than explain the way the process (with its different variations) works and the effects it has on the novel. It may be worth insisting on something I haven't tired of repeating since my first letter: in and of themselves, shifts don't guarantee or indicate anything, and their success or failure in terms of power of persuasion depends on the particular way in which a narrator uses shifts in a specific story: the same process may strengthen a novel's power of persuasion or destroy it.

To conclude, I'd like to remind you of a theory of fantastic literature developed by the great French-Belgian critic and essayist Roger Caillois (in the prologue to his *Anthologie du fantastique*). According to Caillois, true fantastic literature isn't created deliberately; it isn't the result of a conscious effort by an author who sets out to write a fantastic tale. In Caillois's opinion, true fantastic literature requires the spontaneous revelation of incredible, prodigious, fabulous, rationally inexplicable acts, unpremeditated and possibly even unnoticed by the author—it is literature in which the fantastic appears *motu proprio*, as one might say. In other words, these fictions don't tell fantastic stories; they themselves *are* fantastic. This is a very debatable theory, of course, but it is original and rich in possibility, and it provides us with a good way of ending this reflection on shifts, one of whose versions might be—if Caillois isn't too far off track—the autogenerated shift: a shift that would bypass the author, take possession of the text, and set it along a path its creator could never foresee.

Fondly,

Chinese Boxes

Dear Friend,

Another tool that narrators use to endow their stories with power of persuasion is what we might call the "Chinese box" or *matryoshka* technique. How does it work? The story is constructed like those traditional puzzles with successively smaller and smaller identical parts nestled inside each other, sometimes dwindling to the infinitesimal. It should be noted, however, that when a central story begets one or more subsidiary stories, the procedure can't be mechanical (although often it is) if it is to be successful. A creative effect is achieved when a construction of this kind contributes something to the tale—mystery, ambiguity, complexity—that makes it seem necessary, not merely a juxtaposition but a symbiosis or association of elements with a mutually unsettling effect on each other. For example, though one might say that the Chinese box structure of *The Thousand and One Nights*—the collection of famous Arabian stories that upon being discovered and translated into English and French were the delight of

Europe—is often mechanical, it is clear that the puzzle box structure of a modern novel like *A Brief Life* by the Uruguayan writer Juan Carlos Onetti is enormously effective since the extraordinary subtlety of the story and the clever surprises it offers its readers depend almost entirely upon it.

But I'm getting ahead of myself. It would be better to start at the beginning and discuss this technique or narrative device at leisure, moving on later to examine its variants, applications, possibilities, and risks.

I think the best example of the method is the work already cited, a classic of the narrative genre: *The Thousand and One Nights*. Allow me to remind you how the stories are pieced together. To save herself from being beheaded like the other women possessed by the terrible Sultan, Scheherazade tells him stories, scheming so that each night the story is interrupted in such a way that his curiosity about what will happen next—the suspense—makes him prolong her life one more day. In this way, the renowned storyteller manages to survive for a thousand and one nights, and finally the Sultan (won over to the point of addiction by the tales) spares her life. How does the skillful Scheherazade manage to tell so steadily and continuously the interminable series of stories that her life depends on? By using the Chinese box method: fitting stories inside stories through narrative shifts (in time, space, and level of reality). For example: four merchants appear in the story of the blind dervish that Scheherazade tells the Sultan, and one of the merchants tells the other three the story of the leper of Baghdad; in that story, an adventurous fisherman turns up and proceeds to regale a group of shoppers in a market in Alexandria with tales of his maritime exploits. Like Chinese boxes or nesting dolls, each story contains another story subordinate in a first, second, or third degree. Thus, the stories are connected in a system and the whole of the system is enriched by the sum of its parts; each part—each particular story—is enriched, too (or at least affected), according to its dependent or generative role in relation to the other stories.

You yourself can no doubt think of a number of works that feature stories within stories, since the device has long been in use and is very popular; despite being so common, it is always fresh in the hands of a good narrator. At times, as I've said of *The Thousand and One Nights*, the Chinese box method is applied in a somewhat mechanical manner, and the generation of stories by other stories does not trigger significant reverberations within the mother stories (let's call them that). These reverberations occur, for example, in *Don Quixote* when Sancho tells the story—periodically interrupted by Don Quixote's commentary on the way Sancho is telling it—of the shepherdess Torralba (a Chinese box tale in which there is an interaction between the mother story and the daughter story), but other Chinese box narratives, like the excerpt from the novel *The Curious Impertinent* that the priest reads at the inn while Quixote is sleeping, don't work the same way. When speaking of such an episode, it makes more sense to speak of *collage* than of Chinese boxes, since (as is true of many daughter stories or granddaughter stories in *The Thousand and One Nights*) the story has an autonomous existence and doesn't exert a thematic or psychological effect on the story it is contained within (the adventures of Don Quixote and Sancho). Something similar may be said, of course, about another Chinese box classic, *A Captain's Tale*.

The truth is that a lengthy essay could be written on the diversity and variety of Chinese box stories in *Don Quixote*, since Cervantes's genius gave the device a formidable utility, first evident in the invention of the supposed manuscript of Cide Hamete Benengeli of which *Don Quixote* is said be a version or transcription (whether or not this is true is left purposefully unclear). One could say this was a convention worked to death in chivalric novels, all of which pretended to be (or to derive from) mysterious manuscripts discovered in exotic locales. But not even the use of conventions in a novel is empty: it has consequences, sometimes positive, sometimes negative. If we take the existence of Cide Hamete Benengeli's manuscript seriously, the structure of *Don Quixote* is a *matryoshka* of at least four levels of connected histories:

a. The manuscript of Cide Hamete Benengeli, only made known to us in a partial and fractured state, would be the first box. The box immediately subordinate to it, or the first daughter history, is

b. The story of Don Quixote and Sancho, so far as we are allowed to observe it, a daughter story that contains many granddaughter stories (third box), although of a different kind:

c. Stories told among the actual characters, like Sancho's story about the shepherdess Torralba, and

d. Stories incorporated in collage-like fashion and read by the characters; these are freestanding, written stories not intimately linked to the story that contains them, like *The Curious Impertinent* or *A Captain's Tale*.

Now, despite the fact that Cide Hamete Benengeli, quoted and mentioned by the omniscient narrator, appears only outside the bounds of the narrative in *Don Quixote* (though he is still involved in the text, as we noted in our discussion of the spatial point of view), we must step back even further and point out that since he is quoted, his manuscript can't be discussed as the first level, the foundational reality of the novel—the progenitor of all the other stories. If Cide Hamete Benengeli speaks and airs his opinions in the first person in his manuscript (which he does, according to the quotations cited by the omniscient narrator), it is obvious that he is a narrator-character, which means he is part of a story that only in rhetorical terms may be considered self-generated (this, of course, is a structural fiction). All stories told from a point of view in which the narrative space and the narrator's space coincide are also contained by an initial Chinese box outside fictional reality: the hand that writes, inventing (in a first instance) its narrators. Once we become conscious of that first hand (and only hand, since we know Cervantes had only one arm), we must accept that the Chinese boxes of *Don Quixote* are actually four superimposed realities.

The passage from one of these realities to another—from a mother story to a daughter story—constitutes a shift, as you will have noticed. When I say "a" shift, though, I must immediately contradict myself, since the reality is that in many cases a Chinese box story is the result of several simultaneous shifts: in space, time, and level of reality. Let's take a look, for example, at the impressive Chinese box system that *A Brief Life* by Juan Carlos Onetti is built on.

From a technical point of view, this magnificent novel, one of the subtlest and most artful ever written in Spanish, revolves entirely around the artifice of the Chinese box, which Onetti manipulates masterfully to create a world of delicate superimposed and intersecting planes, in which the boundary between fiction and reality (between life and dreams or desires) is dissolved. The novel is narrated by a narrator-character, Juan María Brausen, who lives in Buenos Aires and is tormented by the idea that his lover, Gertrudis, who has cancer, has lost a breast; he also spies on and fantasizes about a woman, Queca, and is trying to write a screenplay. All of this makes up the basic reality or first box of the story. The tale slides in a surreptitious manner, however, toward Santa María, a small provinicial city on the banks of the Río de la Plata, where a doctor in his forties, a shady character, sells morphine to one of his patients. Soon we discover that Santa María, the doctor Díaz Grey, and the mysterious morphine addict are all figments of Brausen's imagination and represent a second level of reality in the story; Díaz Grey is really a kind of alter ego for Brausen, and his morphine-addict patient is a projection of Gertrudis. This is how the novel unfolds, shifting (in space and level of reality) between these two worlds or Chinese boxes and swinging the reader from Buenos Aires to Santa María and back again. Though disguised by the realist-seeming prose and the effectiveness of the technique, these comings and goings are a voyage between reality and fantasy, or, if you prefer, between objective and subjective worlds (Brausen's life and the stories he elaborates). This Chinese box setup isn't the only one in the novel. There is another, parallel one. Queca, the woman Brausen is spying on, is a prostitute who receives clients in the apartment next door to his in Buenos Aires. The story involving Queca takes place—or so it seems at first—on an objective plane like Brausen's own, although it reaches the reader through the medium of the narrator's testimony, and the narrator is a Brausen who must imagine much of what Queca is doing (he hears her but can't see her). And then, at a certain moment—one of the cruxes of the novel and one of its most effective shifts—the reader discovers that the crooked Arce, Queca's pimp, who ends up murdering her, is also really another of Brausen's alter egos, just like Dr. Díaz Grey, a character (partially or totally—this is unclear) created by Brausen—that is to say, someone who exists on a different plane of reality. This second Chinese box is parallel to the Santa María box and coexists with it but it isn't identical, because unlike the Santa María subplot, which is entirely imaginary—the place and its characters existing only in Brausen's imagination—the second box is halfway between reality and fiction, between objectivity and subjectivity: Brausen has added invented elements to a real character (Queca) and her surroundings. Onetti's formal mastery—his writing and the architecture of the story— makes the novel seem to the reader a homogenous whole without internal rifts, even though it is composed, as we've noted, of different planes and levels of reality. The Chinese boxes of *A Brief Life* aren't mechanical. Thanks to them we discover that the true subject of the novel isn't Brausen's story but something vaster, involving shared human experience: the way people retreat into fantasy and fiction in order to enrich their lives, and the way fictions created in the mind are built on the little occurrences of daily life. Fiction is not life as it is lived but a different life, conjured out of the materials supplied by life; without fiction, real life would be a paler and drearier affair.

More later,

The Hidden Fact

DEAR FRIEND,

Ernest Hemingway says somewhere that at the beginning of his writing career it suddenly occurred to him that he should leave out the central event of the story he was writing (his protagonist hangs himself). And he explains that with this decision he discovered a narrative technique that he would later use often in his stories and novels. In fact, it is no exaggeration to say that Hemingway's best stories are full of significant silences; the narrator causes pieces of information to vanish, managing nonetheless to give the missing data an eloquent and insistent presence in readers' imaginations, contriving it so that readers fill in the blanks with their own hypotheses and conjectures. I'll call this technique "the hidden fact" and quickly make clear that although Hemingway gave it a personal twist and used it often (and sometimes masterfully), he hardly invented it, since it is a process as old as the novel itself.

But the truth is that few modern authors have employed it with the same audacity as the author of *The Old Man and the Sea*. Remember "The Killers," an excellent story and perhaps Hemingway's most famous? At its heart is a big question mark: Why do the two outlaws with sawed-off shotguns who come into a little lunchroom called Henry's in the middle of nowhere want to kill the Swede Ole Andreson? And why, when the young Nick Adams warns him that there are a pair of killers after him, does the mysterious Andreson refuse to flee or inform the police, resigning himself calmly to his fate? We'll never know. If we want answers to those two crucial questions, we have to make them up ourselves on the basis of the few facts allotted us by the omniscient and impersonal narrator: before moving to town, Andreson seems to have been a boxer in Chicago, where he did something (something wrong, he says) that sealed his fate.

The hidden fact, or narration by omission, can't be gratuitous or arbitrary. It is vital that the narrator's silence be meaningful, that it have a definite influence on the explicit part of the story, that it make itself felt as an absence, and that it kindle the curiosity, expectations, and fantasies of the reader. Hemingway was a great master of technique, as is evident in "The Killers," a model of narrative economy. Its text is like the tip of an iceberg, a small visible outcropping that gives a glimpse in the lightning flash of its appearance of the complex mass of detail it rests on and is then immediately snatched from the reader's view. To tell by keeping quiet, through allusions that turn the trick into a promise and force the reader to actively intervene in the construction of the story with conjectures and suppositions: this is one of the most common ways narrators succeed in bringing their stories to life and thereby endow them with power of persuasion.

Remember the piece of information hidden in *The Sun Also Rises*, Hemingway's best novel as far as I'm concerned? Yes, the impotence of narrator Jake Barnes. It is never explicitly referred to but grows gradually evident—I'd almost say that the reader, goaded by what he reads, imposes it on the character—out of a telling silence, a strange physical distance, Jake's chaste relationship with the beautiful Brett, whom he clearly loves and who without a doubt also loves him or could have loved him if not for some obstacle or impediment of which we are never precisely informed. Jake Barnes's impotence is an implicit silence, an absence that becomes striking as the reader notices and is surprised by the unusual and contradictory way Jake Barnes relates to Brett, until the only way of explaining it is by realizing (or inventing?) his impotence. Although it is silenced, or maybe precisely because it is silenced, that hidden bit of information bathes the story of *The Sun Also Rises* in a very particular light.

Jealousy is another novel in which an essential element— the main character, no less—is omitted from the story, but in such a way that his absence is projected in the book and felt at every instant. *Jealousy*, which doesn't really have a plot, exhibits the signs or symptoms of a story that we can't quite grasp. We are obliged to reconstruct it the way archaeologists reconstruct the palaces of Babylon from a handful of stones that have been buried for centuries, the way zoologists piece

together prehistoric dinosaurs and pterodactyls from a clav-
icle or a metacarpus. We may safely say that the novels of
Robbe-Grillet—all of them—are based on hidden facts. In
Jealousy, though, the procedure works particularly well, since
in order for the story to make sense it is essential that the
absence in question, the central abolished self, make itself
present and take shape in the consciousness of the reader.
Who is this invisible being? A jealous husband, as the title of
the book ambiguously suggests: someone who, possessed by
the demon of suspicion, spies assiduously on his wife's
movements without being noticed. The reader doesn't know
this for sure; he deduces it or invents it, taking his cue from
the narrator's obsessive, deranged stare devoted to the mad
minute scrutiny of the woman's smallest movements, gestures, and errands. Who is this mathematical observer? Why
does he subject his wife to this visual harassment? The novel
does not reveal the hidden information as it progresses, and
the reader must clear up the mystery on his own, with the
few clues the story provides. These key hidden facts—elimi-
nated forever from the novel—may be called *elliptic*, to differentiate them from facts that are only temporarily hidden
from the reader, displaced in the novel's chronology in order
to create anticipation and suspense, as in mystery novels,
which reveal the identity of the assassin only at the end.
These facts that are only hidden for a while—or temporarily
relocated—may be called *anastrophic*, anastrophe, as you'll
recall, being a poetic device in which a word in a line of
poetry is displaced for reasons of euphony or rhyme. ("Let

me not to the marriage of true minds / admit impediments" instead of the usual order: "Let me not admit impediments to the marriage of true minds.")*

The most remarkable piece of hidden information in a modern novel might be the information omitted from Faulkner's gothic *Sanctuary*, in which the crux of the story—the deflowering of the young and foolish Temple Drake by Popeye, an impotent, psychopathic gangster who uses a corncob—is displaced and dissolved into rivulets of information that allow the reader, little by little and retroactively, to piece together the terrible scene. It is out of this abominable silence that the atmosphere of *Sanctuary* radiates: a climate of savagery, sexual repression, fear, prejudice, and barbarism that gives symbolic significance to Jefferson, Memphis, and the story's other settings, marking them as places of evil and associating them with the ruin and fall of man, in the biblical sense of the term. When faced with the horrors of the novel— the rape of Temple is only one of them; there is also a hanging, a lynching, several killings, a wide-ranging display of moral degradation—we understand that they arise not from the transgression of human laws but from the victory of infernal powers, from the defeat of good by a spirit of perdition that has taken over the earth. *Sanctuary* seethes with hidden information. Besides the rape of Temple Drake, important

*Shakespeare's Sonnet 116 is quoted here in place of Spanish Golden Age poet Luis de Góngora's first eclogue ("Era del año la estación florida . . ."). [*Tr.*]

incidents like the killing of Tommy and Red or facts like Popeye's impotence are silences at first: only retroactively are these blanks filled in. Then, supplied with the information hidden in anastrophe, the reader begins to understand what has happened and to establish the true chronology of events. Not just in this story but in all his stories, Faulkner was the consummate master of hidden information.

For a final example, I'd like to skip back five hundred years to one of the best medieval novels of chivalry: *Tirant Lo Blanc* by Joanot Martorell, a book I keep by the side of my bed. In it, Martorell manipulates hidden information—anastrophic or elliptic—as dexterously as the best modern novelist. Let's see how the narrative material is structured at one of the cruxes of the novel, the "silent marriages" celebrated by Tirant and Carmesina and Diaphebus and Stephanie (in an episode that stretches from the last half of chapter 162 to the middle of 163). This is what happens: Carmesina and Stephanie lead Tirant and Diaphebus into a room of the palace. There, not realizing that Pleasure-of-My-Life is spying on them through a keyhole, the two couples spend the night engaged in love play, innocent in the case of Tirant and Carmesina, much less so in that of Diaphebus and Stephanie. The lovers separate at dawn, and hours later, Pleasure-of-My-Life reveals to Stephanie and Carmesina that she has been witness to their silent marriages.

In the novel, these events appear not in "real" chronological order but discontinuously, the information concealed and revealed in temporal shifts and anastrophic leaps; as a result, the episode is extraordinarily enriched by anecdote. The plot supplies the setup—Carmesina and Stephanie's decision to bring Tirant and Diaphebus into the room—and explains how Carmesina, suspecting that there will be a "celebration of silent marriages," pretends to sleep. The impersonal and omniscient narrator proceeds in "real" chronological order to describe Tirant's astonishment when he sees the beautiful princess, and how he falls to his knees and kisses her hands. Here the first temporal shift or rupture in chronology occurs: "And they uttered many amorous words. When they thought it was time, the knights returned to their quarters." The story leaps into the future, leaving in the gap, the abyss of silence, a sly question: " . . . between love and grief, who could sleep that night?" The narrative next brings the reader to the following morning. Pleasure-of-My-Life gets up, goes into the princess Carmesina's room and finds Stephanie "in no mood to be disturbed." What happened? Why Stephanie's voluptuous abandon? The insinuations, questions, jokes, and gibes of the delicious Pleasure-of-My-Life are really directed at the reader, whose curiosity and prurience are roused. And at last, at the end of this long, clever preamble, Pleasure-of-My-Life reveals that the night before she had a dream in which she saw Stephanie escorting Tirant and Diaphebus into the room. Here the episode's second temporal shift or chronological leap takes place. There is a retreat to the evening before, and through Pleasure-of-My-Life's supposed dream, the reader discovers what happened in the silent marriages. The hidden information is revealed, restoring the episode's integrity. Full integrity? Not quite. As you will have observed, there has been a spatial shift, or change in spatial point of view, as well as a temporal shift, since the voice narrating the silent marriages no longer belongs to the impersonal and eccentric original narrator. It belongs to Pleasure-of-My-Life, a narrator-character whose testimony is not intended to be objective but rather charged with subjectivity (her frank, jocular commentary doesn't just subjectivize the episode; most important, it defuses what would otherwise be the violent story of Stephanie's deflowering by Diaphebus). This double shift—in time and space— therefore turns the episode of the silent marriages into a series of Chinese boxes; that is to say, an autonomous narrative (by Pleasure-of-My-Life) is contained within the general narrative of the omniscient narrator. (Parenthetically, I'll note that *Tirant Lo Blanc* often makes use of the device of Chinese boxes or nesting dolls. The exploits of Tirant over the course of the year and a day that the festivities last in the English court are revealed to the reader not by the omniscient narrator but through the story that Diaphebus tells the count of Vàroic; the capture of Rhodes by the Genoans is made known in a story that two knights of the French court tell Tirant and the duke of Brittany; and the adventure of the merchant Gaubedi is revealed in a story with which Tirant regales the Widow Reposada.) In this way, then, after examining just one episode of a classic narrative, we discover that resources and processes that often seem as if they must be modern inventions because of the showy use contemporary writers make of them are really part of our novelistic heritage, since classic narrators were already using them with assurance. What the moderns have done in most cases is to polish, refine, or experiment with new possibilities implicit in narrative systems that are often manifest in the most ancient written samples of fiction.

Before finishing this letter, I think it might be worthwhile to make a general observation—relevant to all novels—about an innate characteristic of the genre, from which the Chinese box technique is derived. The written part of any novel is just a piece or fragment of the story it tells: the fully developed story, embracing every element without exception—thoughts, gestures, objects, cultural coordinates, historical, psychological, and ideological material, and so on that presupposes and contains the *total* story—covers infinitely more ground than is explicitly traveled in the text, more ground than any novelist, even the wordiest and most prolific, with the least sense of narrative economy, would be capable of covering in his text.

To underscore the inevitably partial nature of all narrative discourse, the French novelist Claude Simon—intending to poke fun at realist literature's conviction that it could reproduce reality—set out to describe a pack of Gitanes. What qualities should the description include in order to be realist? he asked himself. The packet's size, color, content, inscriptions, and the material it was made of were necessary, of course. Would that be enough? In a totalizing sense, no. In order not to leave out any important piece of information, the description would also have to include a meticulous report on the industrial processes involved in the making of the packet and the cigarettes it contained, and—why not?—the systems of distribution and marketing that got them from the producer to the consumer. Once this was done, would the description of the pack of Gitanes be complete? Not even close. The consumption of cigarettes isn't an isolated act: it is the result of the evolution of habits and the introduction of fashions; it is inextricably bound up with social history, mythology, politics, lifestyle. And on the other hand, it is a practice—a habit or vice—on which publicity and economic life exert a definite influence and that has certain effects on the health of the smoker. Following the thread of this demonstration as it progresses to ridiculous extremes, it is not difficult to conclude that the description of even the most insignificant object, if extended in a totalizing manner, leads purely and simply to a utopic proposition: the description of the universe.

Something similar may doubtless be said about fiction. If, theoretically, a novelist didn't impose certain limits when he set out to tell a story (if he didn't resign himself to hiding certain bits of information), his story wouldn't have a beginning or an end but would somehow end up connecting itself with all possible stories and become that chimeric totality: the infinite imaginary universe where all fictions coexist and are intimately linked.

If you accept the supposition that a novel—or rather, a fiction set down in writing—is just a part of a full story from which the novelist finds himself inevitably obliged to eliminate much information because it is superfluous, dispensable, or because it gets in the way of information that he does make explicit, one must nevertheless differentiate between information excluded because it is obvious or useless and the hidden information I refer to in this letter. That is, *my* hidden information isn't obvious or useless. On the contrary, it has a function and plays a role in the narrative scheme, and that is why its elimination or displacement has an effect on the story, producing reverberations in the plot or points of view.

Finally, I'd like to repeat a comparison I once made in discussing Faulkner's *Sanctuary*. Let's say that the *full* story of a novel (including all selected and omitted facts) is a cube and that, once the superfluous pieces of information and the bits omitted deliberately in order to obtain a specific effect are carved away, each particular novel takes on a certain form. That object, that sculpture, is an expression of the artist's originality. It has been shaped with the help of many different tools, but there is no doubt that the hidden fact (if you can't come up with a more appealing name for the device) is one of the most valuable and widely used instruments for cutting away material until the desired beautiful and persuasive form emerges.

Fondly, and until next time,

Communicating Vessels

Dear Friend,

In order for us to discuss this final procedure, involving "communicating vessels" (later I'll explain what I mean by the term), I'd like us to revisit together one of the most memorable episodes of *Madame Bovary*. I refer to the agricultural fair of chapter 8 in the second part of the novel, a scene that is in fact composed of two (or even three) different story lines braided together, each shadowing and in a certain fashion modifying the others. Because of the way the scene is structured, the different events, joined in a system of communicating vessels, exchange material, and an interaction is established among them, causing the episodes to merge into a whole that makes them something more than mere juxtaposed story fragments. A system of communicating vessels operates when the sum of an episode is something more than its parts—and that is true of Flaubert's fair.

Here we have, in scenes interwoven by the narrator, a description of the day the farmers exhibit produce and animals from their farms and celebrate the harvest; the authorities make speeches and award medals; and at the same time, in the council chamber on an upper floor of the town hall, which overlooks the festivities, Emma Bovary listens as Rodolphe woos her with fiery declarations of love. The seduction of Madame Bovary by her noble suitor is perfectly able to stand alone as a scene, but, interwoven as it is with the speech of the councillor Lieuvain, a complicity is established between it and the minor goings-on of the fair. The episode acquires another dimension, another texture, until it might just as well be said that the villagers' celebration takes place below the window where the soon-to-be lovers exchange vows of love: presented alongside their encounter, the fair seems less grotesque and pathetic than it would without the softening effect of such a delicate filter. We are pondering here a very nuanced subject, one that has nothing to do with simple action but rather with finely calibrated ambiance and the emotional and psychological essences that emanate from a story. It is in this context that the system of communicating vessels is most effective, so long as it is handled well.

The whole description of the agricultural fair in *Madame Bovary* is witheringly sarcastic, underscoring to the point of cruelty the human stupidity (*la bêtise*) that fascinated Flaubert, his scorn reaching its height with the appearance of Catherine Leroux, a little old woman who receives an award for her fifty-four years of work in the fields and announces that she will give the prize money to the priest so he will say masses for her soul. If all the poor farmers seem, in Flaubert's description, to be mired in a dehumanizing routine that strips them of sensitivity and imagination and makes them dull figures, thoroughly common and conventional, the authorities are shown in an even worse light as garrulous, blatantly ridiculous nonentities in whom hypocrisy and spiritual duplicity seem primordial character traits, as expressed in the empty and trite utterances of the councillor Lieuvain. But this picture, painted so dark and remorseless that it is hardly credible (and suggests a possible failure of the episode's power of persuasion), only emerges when we analyze the agricultural fair on its own, disassociated from the seduction to which it is viscerally linked. In reality, tangled up as it is with an episode that serves as an escape valve for its vitriolic irony, the sarcastic ferocity of the fair scene is considerably tempered. The sentimental, light, romantic air that is introduced by the seduction establishes a subtle counterpoint, which fosters verisimilitude. And the sunny element of the country fair, presented with exaggerated and humorous irony, also has, reciprocally, a moderating effect, correcting the excesses of sentimentalism—especially the rhetorical excesses—that characterize the episode of Emma's seduction. Without the presence of a very powerful "realist" factor—the presence of the farmers and their cows and pigs in the square down below—the lovers' dialogue, brimming with the clichés and commonplaces of the romantic lexicon, would perhaps dissolve into fantasy. Thanks to the system of communicating vessels that merges the two scenes, the rough edges that might have interfered with each episode's power of persuasion are smoothed and the narrative unity is actually enriched by the resulting amalgam, which gives the chapter a rich and original character.

At the heart of the whole created by the communicating vessels linking the country fair and the seduction, it is possible to establish still another subtle counterpoint—this one on a rhetorical level—that contrasts the mayor's remarks in the square with the romantic words that Emma's seducer whispers in her ear. The narrator weaves the speeches together intending (entirely successfully) that the two—which unspool in a double strand of political and romantic stereotypes—should alternately drown each other out, introducing an ironic perspective without which the tale's power of persuasion would be reduced to a minimum or vanish completely. We may therefore conclude that a second set of specific communicating vessels is enclosed within the general set, reproducing in miniature the overarching structure of the episode.

Now we may attempt a definition of communicating vessels. Two or more episodes that occur at different times, in different places, or on different levels of reality but are linked by the narrator so that their proximity or mingling causes them to modify each other, lending each, among other qualities, a different meaning, tone, or symbolic value than they might have possessed if they were narrated separately: these are communicating vessels. Their mere juxtaposition is not enough, of course, for the procedure to work. The decisive factor is a "communication" between two episodes set side by side or merged in the text by the narrator. The communi-

124

cation may be minimal, but if it doesn't exist at all it is impossible to speak of communicating vessels, since, as we have noted, the unity that this narrative technique establishes makes an episode composed this way always more than the sum of its parts.

The most subtle and daring case of communicating vessels may be that of Faulkner's *The Wild Palms*, a novel that tells, in alternating chapters, two separate stories: one a tragic tale of passionate (and ill-fated adulterous) love and the other that of a convict who in the wake of a devastating natural disaster, a flood that lays waste a vast region, struggles mightily to return to prison, where the authorities, since they don't know what to do with him, sentence him to even more years in prison—for trying to escape! The plots of these two stories never mix, though at a certain point in the story of the lovers there is a reference to the flood and the convict; nevertheless, because of the physical proximity of the protagonists, the language of the narrator, and a certain climate of excess—passionate love in one case, and in the other the fury of the elements and the suicidal integrity that drives the convict to keep his word and return to prison—a kind of resemblance is established. Borges, with the intelligence and precision that never failed him in his literary criticism, put it best: "Two stories that never intersect but somehow complement each other."

Julio Cortázar experiments with an interesting variation on the system of communicating vessels in *Hopscotch*, a novel that takes place, as you may recall, in two settings, Paris

("From the Other Side") and Buenos Aires ("From This Side"), between which it is possible to establish a certain chronology (the Parisian episodes precede the Buenos Aires episodes). At the beginning of the book, there is an author's note suggesting two different possible readings: one (let's call it the traditional one) begins with the first chapter and proceeds in the usual order; the other skips from chapter to chapter, following the directions given at the end of each episode. Only if the reader chooses this second option does he or she read the whole text of the novel; if the first is chosen, a full third of *Hopscotch* is excluded. This third—"From Diverse Sides (Expendable Chapters)"—is not made up of episodes created by Cortázar or narrated by his narrators; it consists of texts and quotations from other sources or, when the material is by Cortázar, of freestanding texts without a direct plot relationship to the story of Oliveira, La Maga, Rocamadour, and the other characters of the "realist" story (if it is not incongruous to use that term to describe *Hopscotch*). They are pieces of a collage that, in its communicating vessel relationship with the novelistic episodes, is intended to add a new dimension— a dimension we might call mythical or literary, an extra rhetorical level—to the story of *Hopscotch*. This, very clearly, is what the counterpointing of "realist" episodes and collage is meant to achieve. Cortázar had already used this system in his first published novel, *The Winners*. In it, he interweaves the adventures of the passengers of the ship on which the story is set with some odd monologues by Persio, a principal character—abstract, metaphysical, sometimes abstruse reflections meant to add a mythical dimension to the "realist" story (though in this case too, as always with Cortázar, it is inadequate to speak of realism).

But it is above all in some of his stories that Cortázar uses the communicating vessel scheme with true mastery. Allow me to remind you of the small marvel of technical craftsmanship that is "The Night Face Up." Remember it? The protagonist, who has been in a motorcycle accident on the streets of a big modern city—almost certainly Buenos Aires—undergoes an operation and, in what at first seems merely a nightmare, is transferred in a temporal shift from the hospital bed where he is convalescing to a precolonial Mexico in the throes of a *guerra florida*, when Aztec warriors hunted for human victims to sacrifice to their gods. From this point on, the story is built on a system of communicating vessels, alternating between the hospital ward where the protagonist is recovering and the remote precolonial night in which in the guise of a Moteca he first flees and then falls into the hands of his Aztec pursuers, who bring him to the pyramid where he is sacrificed with many other victims. The counterpoint is achieved by subtle temporal shifts that, in what we might call a subliminal way, cause the two realities—the present-day hospital and the precolonial jungle—to approach and somehow contaminate each other. Until, at the final crux—which involves another shift, this time not just temporal but in level of reality—the two times merge and the character is in fact not the motorcyclist being operated on in a modern city but a primitive Moteca who, seconds before the priest rips his heart out to appease the bloodthirsty gods, has a visionary glimpse of a future of cities, motorcycles, and hospitals.

Another narrative gem by Cortázar, "The Idol of the Cyclades," is a very similar story, though it is structurally more complex. In it Cortázar uses communicating vessels in an even more original way. Here, too, the story takes place in two different temporal realities, one contemporary and European (a Greek island in the Cyclades and a sculpture workshop on the outskirts of Paris) and one ancient, at least five thousand years old (the primitive civilization of the Aegean, a society of magic, religion, music, sacrifices, and rites that archaeologists have long been trying to reconstruct from the fragments—utensils, statues—that have come down to us). But in this story, past reality filters into the present in a more insidious and unobtrusive way, first through an Aegean statuette that two friends, the sculptor Somoza and the archaeologist Morand, find in the valley of Skoros. Two years later, the statuette sits in Somoza's workshop, and Somoza has made many copies of it, not for aesthetic purposes but because he believes that by doing so he'll be able to transport himself to the time and culture that produced it. In the story's present, in which Morand and Somoza confront each other in the latter's workshop, the narrator seems to insinuate that Somoza has gone mad and that Morand is the sane one. But all of a sudden, at the story's amazing conclusion, when Morand winds up killing Somoza, performing ancient magic rituals on his cadaver, and preparing to sacrifice his own wife, Thérèse, we discover that in fact the little statue has possessed both protagonists, turning them into men of the age and culture that made it, an age that has burst violently into a modern-day present that believed it had buried it forever. In this case, the communicating vessels aren't symmetric as they are in "The Night Face Up," with its balanced counterpoint. Here, the incursions of the remote past are more spasmodic, fleeting, until the splendid final crux—when we see the cadaver of Somoza naked with the ax sunk in his forehead, the little statue smeared with his blood, and Morand, naked too, listening to wild flute music and waiting for Thérèse with his ax raised—makes us realize that the past has entirely subsumed the present, subjecting it to its barbaric and ceremonial magic. By linking two different times and cultures in a narrative unity, the communicating vessels of both stories cause a new reality to be born, one qualitatively different from the mere composite of the two that are merged in it.

And although it seems impossible, I believe that with this explanation of communicating vessels we may conclude our discussion of the tools and principal techniques that novelists use to construct their fictions. There may be others, but I, at least, haven't come across them. The ones that leap out at me from the page (and the truth is, of course, that I don't go searching for them with a magnifying glass, since I'd rather read novels than autopsy them) seem to me likely to be related to one or another of the methods of composition of the stories that have been the subject of these letters.

Fondly,

By Way of a P.S.

DEAR FRIEND,

Just a few lines as a kind of farewell, to reiterate something I've already expressed many times in the course of our correspondence as, spurred on by your stimulating missives, I've tried to describe some of the tools that good novelists use to cast the kind of spell that keeps readers in thrall. And that is that technique, form, discourse, text, or whatever you want to call it (pedants have come up with many names for something that any reader could identify with ease) is a seamless whole. To isolate theme, style, order, points of view, et cetera, in other words, to perform a vivisection, is always, even in the best of cases, a form of murder. And a corpse is a pallid and misleading stand-in for a living, breathing, thinking entity not in the grip of rigor mortis or helpless against the onset of decay.

What do I mean by this? Not, of course, that criticism is useless and unnecessary. On the contrary, criticism can be a very valuable guide to the world and ways of an author, and sometimes a critical essay is itself a creative work, no less than a great novel or poem. (Off the top of my head, here are a few examples: *Studies and Essays on Góngora* by Dámaso Alonso, *To the Finland Station* by Edmund Wilson, *Port Royal* by Sainte-Beuve, and *The Road to Xanadu* by John Livingston Lowes: four very different kinds of critical works, but all of them equally valuable, illuminating, and original.) At the same time, it seems to me of the utmost importance to make it clear that criticism in and of itself, even when it is most rigorous and inspired, is unable to entirely account for the phenomenon of creation, to explain it in its totality. A successful fiction or poem will always contain an element or a dimension that rational critical analysis isn't quite able to encompass. This is because criticism is a labor of reason and intelligence, and in literary creation other factors, sometimes crucial to the work—intuition, sensitivity, divination, and even chance—intervene and escape the very finest nets of literary criticism. That is why no one can teach anyone else to create; at most, we may be taught to read and write. The rest we must teach ourselves, stumbling, falling, and picking ourselves up over and over again.

My dear friend: what I am trying to say is that you should forget everything you've read in my letters about the structure of the novel, and just sit down and write.

Good luck to you.

LIMA, MAY 10, 1997

Index of Names and Works